The Unity
of the
Hebrew Bible

The Unity of the Hebrew Bible

DAVID NOEL FREEDMAN

Distinguished Senior Faculty Lecture Series
College of Literature, Science, and the Arts
The University of Michigan

Ann Arbor
THE UNIVERSITY OF MICHIGAN PRESS

First paperback edition 1993
Copyright © by the University of Michigan 1991
All rights reserved
Published in the United States of America by
The University of Michigan Press
Manufactured in the United States of America

1994   1993   4   3   2

This book presents the 1987–88 Distinguished Senior Faculty Lectures
of the College of Literature, Science, and the Arts,
The University of Michigan

Library of Congress Cataloging-in-Publication Data

Freedman, David Noel, 1922–
    The unity of the Hebrew Bible / David Noel Freedman.
        p.   cm. — (Distinguished senior faculty lecture series)
    Written version of the three talks given in March 1988 at the U.
of Michigan.
    Includes bibliographical references and index.
    ISBN 0-472-10245-1 (alk. paper) — ISBN 0-472-08241-8 (pbk. : alk. paper)
    1. Bible. O.T.—History.   I. Title.   II. Series.
BS1170.2.F74   1991
221.6′6—dc20   91-30874
                                                              CIP

A CIP catalogue record for this book is available from the British Library.

Preface

This book is the written version of three talks given in the Distinguished Faculty Lectureship series at the University of Michigan in March 1988. Although the objective and the substance of the talks remain the same, there are many differences in detail and coloring. These differences are the result of both the shift from oral to written form, and of my reflection on and reaction to the numerous critical comments and queries posed by several readers. Naturally, I hope that the revisions represent an improvement over the original presentation. In any case, this book reflects the ideas I now hold on the subject.

The subject, "The Unity of the Hebrew Bible," was suggested by several recent works on the Bible by a variety of authors who have attempted to trace or demonstrate some unifying or unitary theme throughout the Bible, thus producing a sense of unity in the midst of the obvious heterogeneity and disparity of the Bible's component parts. To what extent they may have succeeded or failed will depend more on the point of view or underlying attitude of the reader than on what these authors actually accomplished in sorting out and putting together the many books that make up the Scriptures. I, like the other authors, must work primarily with the biblical materials, as we lack other sources. My objective has been to reconstruct or describe a rational process by which the admittedly varied and disparate materials in the Bible were consciously and purposefully put together into a complete work by a compiler or an editor working either alone or with a small group of advisers. The unity I am interested in consists in the organization, arrangement, and amalgamation of the different individual literary entities into the whole that we call the Hebrew Bible—and the process by which that feat was achieved.

In order to pursue this objective, I have adopted two working principles, both elementary, easily understood, and while hardly self-evident, nevertheless quite serviceable:

In the Bible, historical narratives generally come down to the time of the author(s); therefore the latest episodes recorded are roughly contemporary with the writer(s) of the stories. Put another way, the work is composed or completed shortly after the last of the stories is finished, and the work may be dated accordingly. A significant burden of proof rests with those who wish to extend the period between the end of the narrative and the composition of the work.

Because we lack external data regarding the composition and publication of biblical books, it is necessary to use internal criteria in making inferences and drawing conclusions concerning the circumstances under which the different books and larger groupings of the Hebrew Bible were compiled and completed. For me, a primary indicator for larger groupings within the Hebrew Bible is symmetry—symmetry defined by structures and numbers, usually of a simple binary or bilateral kind. When symmetry is established or confirmed by examination, it must be the result of conscious planning and deliberate decisions. Therefore I contend that the selection, arrangement, and organization of the books of the Hebrew Bible follow from the deliberate and purposeful decisions and actions of an individual or a small group of people at a particular time and in a particular place, thus producing a unified whole. The purpose of this book is to explore the circumstances under which that process came to fruition, and to determine so far as possible just who was responsible, and when and where and why.

Working through the Hebrew Bible on the basis of these principles, I conclude that this work—with the notable exception of the Book of Daniel, which is admittedly a product in its present form of a much later period—was put together and arranged in much the shape that it has today by a small group of scholars toward the end of the fifth century B.C.E. There is good reason to accept the tradition that the Scribe Ezra (and the Provincial Governor Nehemiah) had much to do with the outcome.

In spite of the modest size of this book, many hands besides mine have had a role in assembling the finished product, and it is altogether fitting that I acknowledge the very substantial help that I have received from various quarters:

Peter Steiner, dean of the College of Literature, Science, and the Arts, who with members of the selection committee chose me to give the initial lectures. I am deeply grateful for this honor and also for the challenge and stimulus to present controversial and original ideas—first in oral form, and after some withering criticism from the same source, to express in written form my reasoned and seasoned views on the subject.

Eugene Nissen, assistant dean of the College of Literature, Science, and the Arts, who encouraged me to put the lectures in written, even publishable form, and who was the first outside reader of the finished document. Fortunately, he expressed general approval of the contents, although he voiced certain reservations. His response encouraged me to go on with the work and to make numerous changes along the way.

Dr. Colin Day, director of the University of Michigan Press, who invited me to submit my manuscript for consideration by the Press after earlier plans for publishing it directly out of the Dean's office fell through. After some misgivings and hesitation, I now agree that it was better to go through the normal and regular process of evaluation and criticism, and I believe the book is better for it.

John Huddlestun, graduate student in the Department of Near Eastern Studies and holder of the Thurnau Fellowship in Biblical Studies. John has done more to make this a learned book than anyone else, including me. He has prepared the footnotes and has otherwise documented some of the less radical and unusual claims made in the text. The more outrageous ones will have to stand supported only by their inherent merit and by the value of the arguments attached to them; John has also supplied numerous data and details intended to enhance the arguments and make them more persuasive. I will, however, take responsibility for the end result.

Dr. Astrid Beck, the program associate in Studies in Religion, who maintained an atmosphere of calm and cool reflection in the office when I was struggling with the most difficult parts of the presentation, whether oral or written. Without her magisterial handling of all the difficult details of organization and arrangement with the helpers mentioned, and the protracted negotiations with the various concerned parties, the project would hardly have gotten off the ground, and it certainly would never have been finished. I am grateful to all those mentioned and also to Thérèse Pasquesi and Jackie Phillips, who contributed time and effort and energy in preparing this manuscript.

Contents

The Primary History

The purpose of this book is to argue for the unity of the Hebrew Bible, to show that it is not just a heterogeneous collection of writings—what remained of Hebrew literature after a thousand years—but that it is a deliberate assemblage conceived and organized by a single mind or by a small group of people. As is the nature of the case, such people are often anonymous, and credit for their accomplishments tends to be assigned to the nearest great name. Having been one of these anonymous editors most of my life, I have a deep interest in and a strong sympathy for these individuals. Among all of those who were responsible for the text of the Hebrew Bible, one personality, however, stands out: the thoroughly recognizable and eminent scribe (or editor) Ezra—a man of distinguished lineage and both traditional and historic importance. A word-picture lingers in the mind: Ezra the Scribe standing before the assembled multitude some time after the middle of the fifth century B.C.E. reading from the Law of Moses (Nehemiah 8).[1] This description occurs toward the end of the combined work known as Ezra-Nehemiah, which, in at least one ancient arrangement, is the last book of the Hebrew Bible. The point is, Ezra is reading from the first books of the Bible, which reflects that the Bible is not only the story of the people of the Bible, i.e., Israel, but that it is also the story of the Bible itself.

Another of the essential biblical personalities is Nehemiah, also of the mid fifth century B.C.E., who, as governor of the Persian province of Judah, was in a position to fund the compilation and publication of the great literary work—and therefore to have the last word on the subject. It may be coincidental that the last words of the Hebrew Bible, which are those of Nehemiah, "Remember me, my God, for good," echo repeated references in the opening paragraphs of the Book of Genesis at the beginning of the Bible: God and good (the words are more alliterative in English than in Hebrew, however).

Before we proceed, however, we must attempt to define or delimit the terms that we are going to use—above all, the term *Bible*. Then we must try to describe and analyze the contents of this great work. We will come back to Ezra and Nehemiah toward the end of this book, just as they came near the end of the process of compiling the books of the Hebrew Bible. One caveat is important. Since the Bible in its various forms and stages has been and still is a canonical or ultimate authority for many people and groups around the world, the questions of authorship, editorship, organization, compilation, and publication are often preempted by a blanket sanction or edict that God, through his spirit, is the author and inspirer of the whole, and that even to ask such mundane questions is irrelevant and irreverent. Without wishing to intrude into the theological sphere at all and, on the contrary, being deferential to personal, private, and public convictions and affirmations, I would insist that whatever its divine dimensions and depths, the Bible from first to last is at the same time an entirely human document. Every word of the Bible was either spoken and then written, or written down by human beings at certain (or uncertain) times and in various places—and it is both possible and proper to address the same questions about the Bible that we would apply to any other work of literature, whether ancient or modern, such as who, what, when, where, how, and certainly why.

Now we may address our first concern—the definition of the term *Bible*. What is the Bible? Whose Bible is it? And which Bible are we talking about? We can restrict the inquiry to the three best-known of the existing Bibles: Jewish, Catholic, and Protestant. In earlier, somewhat simpler times, there was widespread cultural agreement about the preferred English translation of the Bible: the Old and New Testaments of the King James Version. That agreement, however, came at a time when America was overwhelmingly Christian and Protestant by affirmation, and America's culture reflected its religion. It has taken time to discover and consider that the terms *Old Testament* and *New Testament* themselves are tendentious and that the Protestant Bible is the result of a process that involved the amalgamation of materials derived from earlier Bibles.

It is not as though these three Bibles were or are strangers to each other. They overlap and interlock, and each shares important components with the others. Each, however, is also different. As we attempt to analyze and sort out these components, we can introduce the following, somewhat more neutral, terms: the *Hebrew Bible*, which coincides with the Jewish Bible, and the *Greek Bible*, which is equivalent to the Catholic Bible. Historically, the Hebrew Bible came first. It was then, over a period of time, translated into Greek. Included in the Greek Bible were some books, originally written in Hebrew or Aramaic, which were not included in the Jewish Bible, and of which the copies in the original languages have been lost. Hence, these books have survived only in the Greek Bible. The New Testament, originally written in Greek and preserved in that language in the Catholic Bible, was added to all of these books. In the end, the Protestant Bible, compiled centuries later, consisted of the Hebrew Old Testament (Jewish Bible) and the Greek New Testament (derived from the Christian [Catholic] Bible).

We can speak of a threefold Bible with concentric circles or overlapping parts. Thus all three Bibles include the core or basis: the Hebrew Bible or Old Testament. The Protestant Bible adds the New Testament, while the Catholic Bible includes everything in the other two and adds the so-called apocryphal (or deuterocanonical) books of the Old Testament, such as 1 and 2 Maccabees, 1 and 2 Esdras, Tobit, Judith, Ecclesiasticus, and Wisdom.

From this welter of options, I have selected the core Bible, the Hebrew Bible, for various reasons. First, it is recognized as *the* Bible, or part of it, by those who acknowledge the Bible as authoritative; the books of the Hebrew Bible are included in all the Bibles. A more practical reason is that this is the Bible I have studied throughout my career, and as a scholar, I am much better qualified to talk about the Hebrew Bible than the Greek Bible, about the Jewish Bible than either of the Christian ones. Finally, even in these lectures, there is only so much space and time available, and the subject is too large even when limited in this fashion. So we will define the Bible as the Hebrew Bible or the Old Testament.[2]

The next step is to explain the divisions of this great work, and after that we may take up our first topic: the Primary History. Now that we have accurate statistics for the Hebrew Bible, we can be much more precise about the lengths of books, their proportions, and the exact format of the parts and divisions. It will be worthwhile to consider briefly these statistics. In what follows we are speaking only of the Hebrew (and Aramaic) Bible (the Old Testament). There are 305,500 words in the Bible, but we will round that number to 300,000.

Although there are many different ways of dividing and organizing the Hebrew Bible, the best way, in my judgment, is to start with the traditional Jewish divisions as being most in keeping with the character and quality of the material. The Jewish tradition divides the Hebrew Bible into three parts, signified by the acronym *TaNaK*: *Torah* or Law, *Nebi'im* for the Prophets, and *Ketubim* for the Writings. Of these three divisions, the second is divided into two major subdivisions, since it is almost twice the length of the others. The second part, or the Prophetic Corpus, consists of Former Prophets and Latter Prophets. The three major divisions are in turn divided into the many books of the Bible, whose names are familiar to all: Genesis, Exodus, etc., in the Torah; Isaiah, Jeremiah, etc., among the Prophets; and Psalms, Proverbs, Job, etc., as examples of the Writings. Using round numbers, we arrive at the following distribution and proportions:

Torah or Law	5 books	80,000 words
Former Prophets	4 books	70,000 words
Latter Prophets	4 books	72,000 words
Writings	11 books	84,000 words

(From the last group we could subtract one book of 6,000 words, the Book of Daniel, and come out with 78,000 words, but we will address this later.)

The Prophets are almost twice as long as either of the other major subdivisions, and they divide neatly and evenly into two groups of four books each: (1) Joshua through 2 Kings (excluding Ruth); and (2) Isaiah, Jeremiah, Ezekiel, and the Book of the Twelve, i.e., Hosea through Malachi (counted as one book). The Writings, whose name indicates a miscellaneous or catchall category with eleven books, nevertheless can also be described in more precise fashion. There are three major poetic books in this group: Psalms, Job, and Proverbs. Then we have the five *megillot* or rolls, which, while written separately, constitute a single, middle-sized collection comparable to the Twelve Minor Prophets. The *megillot* were always written seriatim on a single scroll. Finally, excepting the Book of Daniel, which requires an independent explanation, there is the Chronicler's Work consisting of two continuous scrolls: 1 and 2 Chronicles and Ezra-Nehemiah.

One further adjustment is indicated. The four parts of the Hebrew Bible, roughly equivalent in size and forming a symmetrical pattern, can (and should be) grouped or arranged in a somewhat different fashion. If we divide the four parts in the middle, then the Former Prophets becomes attached to the Torah to form a single continuous narrative from Genesis through Kings. These nine books (really scrolls) comprise just about 150,000 words, or half of the entire Hebrew Bible. This rearrangement (and it is hardly more than a relabeling, since the nine books—Genesis to

Deuteronomy and Joshua to Kings—remain in exactly the same order as before) reveals the true nature of the initial main and central content of the Bible. I have termed this nine-book collection the Primary History, chiefly because I have never found a name for it in the literature. I have also called it the First Bible because that is what it is. It is central and basic, the core and foundation of the rest of the books, which are related to it, dependent on it, and do not make much sense without it. So, in more than one sense, it constitutes the *Primary* History, and therefore deserves to be discussed before the other parts.[3]

In dealing with biblical books, and with the major divisions within the Hebrew Bible as a whole, we utilize a principle of analysis and evaluation that focuses attention on certain parts in contrast with others in order to isolate elements that identify and emphasize the structure of the work and hence its meaning and importance.

Briefly, the structure of much of the literature is pyramidal and symmetric; it is like a domed building in which the apex is near or at the center, and the opening and closing form a ring or pair of interlocking parts that constitute the foundation. For the Hebrew Bible as a whole, the center comes at the end of the Primary History and at the beginning of the Latter Prophets—at which point the Bible tells of the captivity of the people of Judah, the loss of nationhood, and the destruction of the capital city of Jerusalem and the Temple. In a similar way, if we look at the corpus of Latter Prophets, the same melancholy series of events is at the center, in the latter part of Jeremiah and the first part of Ezekiel. Even in the Writings, with its great diversity of materials, the central point is held by the Book of Lamentations, which, while very brief (five chapters—about 1,500 words), is also devoted entirely and exclusively to those same series of events. We can say, therefore, that the entire Hebrew Bible revolves around that point in time, that historical moment when the life of the nation came to an end, when tragedy struck in multiple blows at the kingdom, at its ruling dynasty, and at the sacred center of worship and service of their

God. Such a decisive event and its enveloping circumstances must have had a powerful effect and pervasive influence over the literature as a whole, and most of what is written in the Bible reflects this unquestioned fact of Israel's (or Judah's) experience.

Although the fall of Jerusalem is in the middle of the Bible (and central to it) and also in middle of the subdivisions (Latter Prophets and Writings), this is clearly not the case with the Primary History. As mentioned, the fall of Jerusalem is where the Primary History ends—not an unimportant location to be sure, but also not the center. We will therefore look for another point of interest and emphasis at the center of the Primary History.

If our contention about the scope and nature of the Primary History has any merit, then we would expect to find some clues about the end of the work at or near the beginning. Such clues would demonstrate that the author/compiler/editor was fully aware of the end of the story from the outset and that this person used appropriate literary devices to demonstrate this awareness. When we look at the first book, Genesis, we note immediately that the story of Abraham and his offspring (in particular Isaac, Jacob, and Jacob's twelve sons, who in a breathtaking sleight of hand between the books of Genesis and Exodus become the twelve tribes of the nation of Israel) is preceded by an elaborate introduction (chaps. 1–11). This introduction is rather grandiose and spacious, much more than would be required for the immediate needs of the story, but entirely appropriate for the "great narrative" that follows in the nine books of the Primary History. These preliminary accounts of Creation and the cosmic and terrestrial adventures and experiences of God and mortals serve several purposes; the chief purpose is to establish the full range of power and authority of the God who is the central and dominant figure of the whole story and the entire Bible, thus ensuring that no one would confuse the almighty God of Genesis 1–11 with the puny and pusillanimous family and nation in which he showed particular and peculiar interest. Israel's unimportant place in the affairs of the world (asserted more than a few times in a form of reverse pride) in no way impinged upon or reduced God's dominant and supreme role in the affairs of all his creatures (including humans), as the opening chapters of Genesis make clear.

But what do these stories tell us about the humans in the picture? Briefly put, they tell successive stories of human disobedience and depravity, of resistance to the will of the Lord God, and of the necessary consequences in punishment and, more specifically, in banishment and exile. These stories are, simply put, successive parables about Israel's experience, its relationship to its God and the consequences of its rebellion against the will of the sovereign Lord. For those writing and reading the finished version of the story, which was published shortly after the last entry at the end of Kings, the linkage would be unmistakable. Adam and Eve in the Garden of Eden is a story of disobedience and rebellion against the commandment of God. The upshot is banishment from the Garden to the life of exile in the world. How could those in captivity in Babylon, as described at the end of Kings, miss the point or fail to compare the story in Genesis with theirs? The next story, that of Cain and Abel, makes essentially the same point. If you are guilty of a crime against a neighbor/brother, then you deserve the same punishment. The sentence, however, is commuted to exile, and thanks to the kindness of a merciful deity, the exile is not without some modest mitigation of its harsh conditions. Although the misery of the exiles is reflected in these stories, they are not without redeeming features, and there are glimmers of hope even for those who have lost homes and land, city and temple, and nation.

The point is even more marked in the story of the Flood, which prescribes a nearly total destruction of the created world as a consequence of sin, corruption, and rebellion. Even as the destruction is generalized to include the whole of humanity, the deliverance of a single family is also articulated so that the dual lesson will not be missed: While this ultimate destruction is richly deserved by those who suffer it, for the handful of survivors there is hope of a future in a newly rebuilt world. Thus there is hope for the survivors in the Babylonian Exile.

The point is driven home in the last of the four stories, the Tower of Babel (the others being the Garden of Eden, Cain and Abel, and the Flood). Without dwelling on the details, I wish to point out that it was from this place, Babel, the city of Babylon, that the immediate ancestors of Abraham set out (Genesis 11–12) on the migration that would end with Abraham's pilgrimage to the land of Canaan. Now, many centuries later (perhaps a millennium or more), the exiles are back in Babylon. Going from Babylon to Babylon may seem like a retrograde journey. After all the time and effort and devotion and dedication, there was precious little, if anything, to show for that struggle for independence and statehood. The exiles were back where they started! But it would not get worse, and when the signal from God came, they could start again. Babylon may have been where the dreams ended, but it is also where they could begin, and they would one day begin again. The use of the word "Chaldeans" (Hebrew *Kasdim*), which in the Primary History is restricted to Genesis and 2 Kings (Genesis 11:28, 31; 2 Kings 24:2, 25:4 passim), reinforces the view that the opening and closing are carefully fitted together to reveal the end from the beginning, and to compel the thoughtful reader to acknowledge that the seeds were planted at the beginning and the fruits were revealed at the end.

But now we must consider the nature of this great literary endeavor that comprises half of the Hebrew Bible: the Primary History. So far as I am aware, it is the first and perhaps the most important and influential prose narrative ever written, preceding, for example, Herodotus and his *History of the Persian Wars* by at least a century. The Primary History may be compared with such a historical work because it constitutes historical writing, although it is perhaps more credulous in some respects than modern historians would require. In other words, although it is not history in the modern sense, it is clearly interested in real people, real places, and real events. There is also a connection with epic poetry of the kind we identify in the *Iliad* and *Odyssey* and, before that, the great cycle of poems associated with Gilgamesh and Enkidu.[4]

Perhaps comparison with the *Iliad* is most appropriate since central to both is the fall of a capital city and the accompanying collapse of a dynasty and kingdom. A principal, perhaps decisive, difference is that the *Iliad* reflects the perspectives of the winners— the Greeks, who finally captured and destroyed Troy—while the biblical account is told from the point of view of the losers, i.e., the people who fought a losing battle and lost everything. The pervasive note of tragedy all through the Hebrew Bible reflects this fundamental difference. Another difference reflected in the Greek epics involves the treatment of the gods, who are many; the scenes depicting them in their heavenly abode, as well as their interaction with human beings, make for considerable excitement and entertainment. In the Bible there is only one God, albeit he is supported by a cast of heavenly helpers and retainers. But much of the conflict among the gods, and the resulting tension and suspense, have been liquidated in the Bible in the interest of monotheism and the moral and ethical relationship between creator and creature that dominates the biblical scene. If the biblical account is short on mythology, it is long on theology, especially the question of theodicy: it confronts the issue of Israel's relationship with God and the historical consequences for the nation, ending in the ruin and exile of its people.

The attempt to interpret historical events and the destiny of nations in terms of moral principles and values may ultimately have raised more questions than such a theory could answer, and in the end may have failed to satisfy the conscience and mind of the keenest thinkers within Israel (and outside of it) and the most sensitive souls. But it did serve to organize, synthesize, and consolidate vast quantities of otherwise amorphous data—data that were the flotsam and jetsam of an equally haphazard polytheism that teetered between the personal petty pleasures and distastes of individual gods and the blind determinism of the fates that never swerved from their course, regardless of pleas, threats, or bribes offered by gods and humans alike.

The Primary History offered both an account of the origin, rise, ascendance, decline, and fall of Israel, and an interpretation of that prolonged and ultimately agonizing experience. Everything hinged on the relationship between creator and creature, the commander and the commanded, the ruler and the ruled. This relationship is described in terms of a variety of covenants or pacts made between God and humanity (or with individuals) through the course of time. We may group them into two classes or categories: (1) those that consist of a divine commitment or promise—unconditional, unilateral, and irrevocable as in the classic and dramatic instance of God's promise to Abraham (recorded in Genesis 15) that there would be unnumbered posterity, nationhood, and territory, and that he would be the source of blessing to the peoples of the world; and (2) those that balance these divine commitments with the more typical or regular covenant of human obligation, whereby the human partner, in this case Israel, is bound to observe the terms of the covenant laid down by the deity and, in a word, be obedient to the commandments.

This latter covenant between God and Israel was mediated by Moses at Mount Sinai and is summarized in the Decalogue, a climactic moment in Israel's history and a matter of central importance to the story. While this episode must come early in the story—in the Book of Exodus, right after Genesis and a long way from Kings (at the end) or Deuteronomy (in the middle)—we can recognize the resourcefulness of the compiler, who generally does not twist the facts or his narrative to accommodate literary niceties or structural objectives, but manages nevertheless to achieve both ends, sometimes in bravura fashion. Thus, while the central event of the giving of the commandments and the ratification of the covenant takes place in Exodus, it is at the midpoint of the Primary History, namely the Book of Deuteronomy, that Moses, near the end of his life, recalls the stirring events that happened at the sacred mountain forty years earlier and recreates them in detail for the reader or listener. The compiler has brought the covenant with its commandments to the center and heart of the total work, reinforcing its meaning and power, while at the same time keeping it where it belongs in the narrative sequence. Needless to say, as modern advertisers know, repetition is the most effective way of inculcating a message and ensuring that it will be heard and remembered.

It is precisely with the Decalogue that I wish to complete this first lecture. The Ten Commandments (Exodus 20:1–17; Deuteronomy 5:1–22) constitute the essence of the covenant demands and summarize the obligation of Israel to its God. The conditions of the covenant require obedience to the will of the God who brought the people out of slavery in Egypt and promise or threaten two kinds of outcome or result. If Israel, individually and collectively, obeys the terms of the covenant, then the promises will be richly fulfilled and the people of Israel will achieve prosperity and security in the land that God is giving to them. Failure to obey, however, will bring dire punishment and the reversal of all the good things received or promised. The commandments are representative of the divine demands and are aimed first at each individual, who is obliged to obey them. The community, at the same time, is also held responsible for the behavior of its members, and must answer to God for them. In other words, the community through its leaders serves as the deputy or agent of the deity and must enforce his laws, administer justice, punish evildoers, and defend the innocent. Failure to carry out these responsibilities constitutes breach of covenant and will bring on the disastrous consequences detailed at length in the Book of Deuteronomy, the centerpiece of the Primary History.

Overall and in general, throughout the Primary History, the author's plan is clear. Although God faithfully carried out his promises and brought his people out of slavery to freedom, out of Egypt and into Canaan, giving them a land and a nation, they nevertheless, and in spite of efforts at different times and places to perform their duty, finally failed. They failed so badly that the sanctions of the covenant were set in motion and in the end they lost their land, their state, their city, and their temple, and ended up in captivity—first the Northern Kingdom (Israel) and then the Southern Kingdom (Judah). They had no one to blame but themselves, and that is where the Primary History ends. Here and there we find a hint that the end is not the end and that a new beginning is possible, but the story itself ends in destruction and captivity.

The evidence for such unifying editorial activity can be seen in the links between the parts of the Primary History that derive from different authors; the further apart such links are, the more likely it is that they reflect the work of an editor, especially at the beginning and the end. Thus editorial touches that connect Genesis with Kings are especially indicative and valuable in pointing to the work of such an editor or compiler. Examples that I have cited elsewhere include the apparent, if superficial, link between the first stories in the Book of Genesis (Adam and Eve, Cain and Abel), both of which deal with punishment for sin or crime, and the fate of the nation at the end of 2 Kings.[5] In these cases the outcome for the disobedient is banishment or exile, precisely the fate of the presumed readers of those stories, who are themselves the subjects of the final chapters of 2 Kings, the exiles in Babylon. The latter city is the subject of the story of the Tower of Babel (Genesis 11), the first narrative after the renewal of life on earth following the Flood. That story supplies the transition to the account of Abraham's family and the beginning of the patriarchal narrative. So what began in Babylon more than a millennium before ends in the same place for Abraham's remote descendants: from Babylon to Babylon provides a neat summary or envelope for the whole of the Primary History. Only a compiler/editor would have achieved explicitly what was only implicit in the separately authored blocks of material.

We could go on with other examples of the editor's art, but let us turn to a more elaborate structural feature that pervades the whole work, cuts across source and authorship lines, and—if sustainable as the work of the compiler—may give us an entirely new perspective on how he managed this vast enterprise. I speak here of "The Nine Commandments."

The Nine Commandments

It is generally agreed that a principal theme of the Primary History is to explain how it happened that Israel—the chosen people of

God who were rescued by him from bondage in Egypt and established in a new homeland, the land of Canaan, to be his nation—lost their independence and their land and ended up in exile far away. While the details of this tragedy, the decline and fall of the two nations, Israel and Judah, are narrated in ideological and political/military terms, if not socioeconomic ones, the overriding theme is that just as Israel was created by God, so it could be and was destroyed by him. Thus, while the deliverance of Israel and its establishment as a nation were the deeds of a gracious God, who acted on the basis of a prior commitment to the Patriarchs beginning with Abraham, the continued existence of the nation, not to speak of its success, security, and prosperity, would depend on its behavior. Specifically, it depended on its adherence to a code of conduct that was both agreeable and pleasing to God and spelled out in the hundreds of rules and regulations—moral and cultic, civic and religious, social, political, and economic—that permeate the pages of the Torah.

These rules and regulations, in turn, are summed up in the Decalogue or Ten Commandments, with which every Israelite must have been familiar.[6] Here, in a word (or the "Ten Words" as they are called in the Bible), is the epitome of the covenant, a summary of the rules by which all Israel is to live under the sovereign rule of God. As Moses in the speeches in Deuteronomy and Joshua in his speeches in Joshua 23–24 make clear, there is both promise and threat in the terms of the covenant: If Israel obeys the laws of the covenant, then all will be well, and Israel will prosper under the aegis of its God; if, however, the people of Israel disobey the commandments and rebel against the authority of their God, then everything will be lost—prosperity, security, nationhood, and land.

Most readers, scholars, and lay people would probably agree with this. Clearly, there are other themes and important features, so far unmentioned, but certainly the interpretation of Israel's history and destiny in this major narrative properly emphasizes Israel's covenant obligation and its persistent and repeated failure to live up to the covenant's central demands.

Now we wish to proceed beyond the commonplace and commonly accepted to something more, something a little more creative and dramatic. Let me try to put myself in the shoes of the editor/compiler, or at his desk, and ask how I can sharpen the focus, highlight the drama of this decline and fall of the nation(s), and bring home to the survivors the necessary if onerous lesson of the past so as to strengthen their resolve in their present affliction and prepare them for something better in the future, a future that will hold out a very similar combination of threat and promise.

I would go about my task in the following manner: first I would point to the Decalogue as the core and center of the covenant. The simplest way to do this is by repetition. The Decalogue is found in both the P(riestly)-Work, or P-Work, (Exodus 20) and the D(euteronomistic)-Work, or D-Work[7] (Deuteronomy 5). Instead of combining or conflating them, we keep them separate, but ingeniously let these works overlap so that the Decalogue appears twice in the story, near the beginning of Israel's march from Egypt to Canaan, and just before the end, after leaving Egypt and before entering Canaan. Therefore, the Decalogue will appear in its proper chronological position in Exodus, but will then be repeated at a later stage in the story, and at a strategic point in the literary structure.

The Book of Deuteronomy, the fifth book, is at the center of the nine books in the narrative sequence and thus serves as the pivot or apex of the entire work. That this is not just a numerical accident or coincidence is shown by the book's contents: Moses, the central figure of the Primary History, dominates the whole book, which is devoted to a series of addresses by this greatest of Israel's leaders toward the end of his life, i.e., his valedictory, which has special authority and power. And in the series of sermons, Moses not only reviews the precedent history of his people (thereby providing legitimate reason to bring in the Ten Commandments, a climactic experience at the beginning of a new era), but also, as a true prophet, he forecasts what is going to happen to the people in the future, depending on their behavior. Thus the Book of Deuteronomy encompasses practically the entire Primary

15

History and deservedly occupies the central and dominant position in the narrative. So the Decalogue is not only at the beginning of national history, but also at the center of the narrative.

We can outline the sequence of events as follows: Israel was delivered from bondage in Egypt and was brought to the sacred mountain, Sinai. There the people were given the Decalogue as a précis of the terms of the covenant. They agreed to the terms, and the covenant was solemnly ratified by sacrifices and a common meal at the mountain (Exodus 24). The rest of the story is told in the succeeding books and is an account of repeated violations of the covenant, interrupted by occasional reversals and reforms, but culminating in the renunciation of Israel by its maker and founder, and the destruction of the nation—first the Northern Kingdom in 722 B.C.E. and then the Southern Kingdom in 587/6 B.C.E.

It is easy to say that according to the authors/editors, Israel, after committing itself to obey the commandments of God, failed to do so; the people broke the Decalogue, the terms of the covenant, and were punished for doing so by the loss of nationhood and their territory, ending up in captivity in Babylon. But we want to make the case more precise, more dramatic and suspenseful, and so we call upon our ingenious and resourceful editor to provide a way through the complex details of a 600-year history from beginning to end. We will suppose that the editor, while constrained by the already written stories and books available to him, will nevertheless shape and organize the story to accomplish the following:

Using the Decalogue as his point of departure, the editor is going to have Israel violate each one of the commandments directly and explicitly. Further, Israel will violate them in order, one by one, and, given the fact that the editor has a group of books (or scrolls) to deal with, one commandment and one violation will be assigned to each book.

With respect to the incidents, each one will be related directly or indirectly, explicitly or implicitly, to the appropriate commandment, and this linkage will be apparent. In addition, wherever possible, the seriousness of the episode will be stressed in such a way as to show how the violation (usually by an individual) nevertheless involved or implicated the whole nation, so that the survival of the latter was put in jeopardy. In each instance, the nation or community was in peril or at risk, and on the verge of disaster. Only through the extraordinary intervention of a leader or the precipitate change of direction on the part of the people was a reason found to spare the people. In each instance, God finally relented and the relationship was patched up. But the threat and warning remain and are strengthened, so that each succeeding violation brings Israel (and Judah) ever closer to destruction. At the end of the string, all (but one) of the commandments will have been violated, and Yahweh's patience will have run out. It is clear that the next violation will bring the decisive judgment that will put an end to the proceedings and the national history of Israel.[8]

That is roughly the scenario we propose. What are the chances that such a pattern and sequence actually occur in the Primary History? And if they do occur, or any portion of them, is that evidence of a guiding editorial hand? We may leave those questions for later discussion and simply point to the evidence in the Primary History as it has been preserved. Since we posit an editor or compiler who is working with existing literary works and not just a collection of bits and pieces, he will be limited in the degree and extent to which he can arrange or rearrange, organize and reorganize, or manipulate his material. Hence we can expect certain deviations and adjustments as the editor, and we, go along. In addition, there are two basic problems that must be faced from the beginning:

There are ten commandments but only nine books. Neither of these basic data can be changed, so an adjustment will be necessary. The editor will have to dissolve or absorb one of the commandments along the way or otherwise account for the discrepancy. The numbers nine and ten are not that far apart, however, so our idea remains an interesting and intriguing one.

The story of covenant-making and covenant-breaking properly begins with the Book of Exodus. While Genesis has covenants and covenant-ceremonies (e.g., with Noah in Genesis 9, and with

Abraham in Genesis 15 and 17), they are not the same as the covenant made at Sinai/Horeb and mediated by Moses, and are not related to the Decalogue. Hence we begin with the second book and must therefore account for the missing book by doubling up the commandments or by some other fashion.

If we can negotiate these difficulties and overcome these and other obstacles, we will not just show our own ingenuity but perhaps expose the hand of our versatile editor. We will note some other disparities or discrepancies elsewhere in the sequence, but surmounting these difficulties will also show how the editor might have handled the problems. Naturally we should not end up with just a collection of adaptations and adjustments. To make the case at all, the bulk of the commandments must come in order, one to a book, and reach a climax in the last (and ninth) book with a violation of the ninth commandment, and the conclusion of the story near at hand.

There is one more preliminary matter to be cleared up before we can proceed to test the hypothesis. As everyone knows, there are several different ways of counting the Decalogue, and the several religious traditions that acknowledge them as authoritative (e.g., Roman Catholic, Lutheran, Jewish) go different ways in assigning the numbers.[9] Since it is a matter of some import, and we don't want to be accused of following or adopting one particular system simply because it fits our requirements better than the others, we will follow what might be called the consensus position to which most scholars adhere. We here list the commandments, with the location of their respective violations, in an abbreviated fashion (asterisks indicate variation in order, see note 9):

The Ten Commandments

Prohibitions			Violations	
Exodus 20		Deuteronomy 5		
Verse 3	APOSTASY	Verse 7	(1)	Exod. 32
4	IDOLATRY	8	(2)	Exod. 32
7	BLASPHEMY	11	(3)	Lev. 24:10–16

Prohibitions			*Violations*	
Exodus 20		Deuteronomy 5		
Verse 8	SABBATH	Verse 12	(4)	Num. 15:32–36
12	PARENTS	16	(5)	Deut. 21:18–21
15	STEALING	19	(8)*	Josh. 7
13	KILLING	17	(6)*	Judg. 19–21
14	ADULTERY	18	(7)*	2 Sam. 11–12
16	FALSE WITNESS	20	(9)	1 Kings 21
17	COVETING	21	(10)	———

The Ten Commandments are given for the first time at Mount Sinai in Exodus 20. The Israelites agree to obey them, and the covenant between God and Israel is ratified in a combination of ceremonies recorded in Exodus 24. Immediately thereafter, Moses goes up the mountain to receive instructions for building the Tabernacle. During his absence, the well-known incident of the Golden Calf takes place (Exodus 32). The episode is described in such a way as to make it clear that the Israelites have violated both of the first two commandments.

1. You shall have no other gods besides me. (Exodus 20:3)
2. You shall not make for yourself an image. (Exodus 20:4)

Not only do they make the Golden Calf, but they speak of it as a god or rather as more than one god:

And they said, "These are your gods, O Israel, who brought you up from the land of Egypt." (Exodus 32:4)

What precisely the plural usage ("thy gods") signifies is not clear (it may be a reflex of the two bull-images at Bethel and Dan in the Northern Kingdom), but the writer represents the people as being guilty of both apostasy and idolatry. It may be observed as well that in certain communions the two commandments are treated as one—indicating, as the Deuteronomist clearly implies, that apostasy and idolatry are really two aspects of the same violation, the abandonment of Yahweh for other gods, who are regularly represented in cultic practice by their images.

For our purposes, it is important to note that we have a double violation in a single event, and thus we have accounted not only for the first two commandments, but also for the first two books of the Primary History. Before continuing, we also wish to point out that the episode in question meets the other norms or requirements that we established earlier. While some are guilty of violating the covenant and others are not (e.g., the Levites), the existence of the community is nevertheless still threatened. God tells Moses that he will wipe out Israel and create a new people from Moses' progeny. It is only after Moses' intercession and a partial slaughter of the guilty apostates that God relents and the community is allowed to live and carry on its activity. And needless to say, the linkage with the Decalogue is direct and immediate. This episode becomes the paradigm for the whole subsequent history of Israel. A violation of any of the commandments is a violation of all of them, indeed of the whole covenant, but the primary category is always expressed in the words *apostasy* and *idolatry*, which in that sense are a digest or summary of the Decalogue— just as the Decalogue is itself a digest of the full range of rules and regulations of the covenant. We want to emphasize that the violations we select and use are rarely unique, and others in the same category occur elsewhere. It would not be difficult to make a list of violations that did not meet our requirements. Remember, we are talking about an editor, a compiler, *not* an originator or author, although I think in the end the case we make is both strong and unique.

In any case, the countdown has begun, and we are ready to proceed to the third book and the third commandment. The third book is Leviticus and the third commandment prohibits the misuse of the name of God, i.e., blasphemy:

You shall not invoke the name of Yahweh your God for falsehood. (Exodus 20:7)

In Leviticus 24:10–16, there is a story about a man whose name is not given but whose pedigree is. His mother was an Israelite, his father an Egyptian. He is charged with blasphemy and is ultimately executed for the violation of the commandment:

> The son of an Israelite woman came out (he was the son of an Egyptian man) in the midst of the Israelites; and the son of the Israelite woman and an Israelite man were in a fight. The son of the Israelite woman cursed the Name, and he committed blasphemy. So they brought him to Moses (the name of his mother was Shelomith the daughter of Dibri of the tribe of Dan). They placed him in custody until the decision of Yahweh would be made known to them. Then Yahweh spoke to Moses as follows: Bring the blasphemer outside the camp and let all those who heard (the blasphemy) place their hands upon his head, and let the entire assembly stone him. And to the Israelites you shall speak as follows: Any man, if he curses his God, then he shall bear (the consequence of) his sin. The one who curses the name of Yahweh shall surely be put to death, and the whole congregation will stone him, the alien resident as well as the native born; whoever curses the Name shall be put to death.

Some have argued that Exodus 20:7 deals not with cursing the name of God as in the above story, but with using the name in oaths, i.e., swearing falsely by Yahweh's name (note, e.g., the rendering of this verse in the Jewish Publication Society's translation; see note 2). However, there is an obvious connection between these two actions in that both involve the utterance and pronunciation of the sacred name of God. That the episode in Leviticus may not reflect the original or perhaps central meaning of the commandment does not affect the case, and may even strengthen my point. That is, we need not assume that the person who composed the Decalogue also wrote the stories and arranged them in the order I have described, and therefore that everything will fit together neatly and nicely. On the contrary, different people with different mentalities are involved, therefore, we should not expect things to fit together in a nice scholarly and scientific manner. Rather, the jointures should be rough, and the expertise of the authors/editors is of a different sort from what we modern scholars do and expect of each other.

While the language used in Leviticus is slightly different from the wording of the commandment, it is clear that the writer has the covenant and the Decalogue in mind. The Ten Commandments are different from the bulk of the regulations in that they do not have a specific penalty attached to them. In this instance, therefore, the guilty party is detained until the matter of punishment has been resolved. The Israelites recognize that there has been a serious breach of the covenant, but neither they nor Moses know how to deal with the matter.

When word is received, it is necessary for the whole community, including those who witnessed the crime, to participate in the act of judgment. In that way, the community is cleared of complicity with the guilty person, and therefore escapes the consequences of this fatal breach of the covenant. While the particular occurrence may seem trivial in comparison with the making of the Golden Calf, the special treatment accorded this passing event shows that the writer (or editor) had in mind the highest level of covenant obligation—the Decalogue.

The fourth book is Numbers and the fourth commandment requires observance of the Sabbath. The commandment reads as follows:

> Remember [in Deuteronomy 5:12, the word is "Observe"] the Sabbath Day to keep it holy. For six days you shall labor and do all your work, but the seventh day is a *sabbath* of Yahweh your God. You shall do no work at all, neither you nor your son nor your daughter, your male or female servant, nor your cattle, nor the alien who is within your gates. (Exodus 20:8)

In Numbers 15:32–36, there is a story about a man who gathered sticks on the Sabbath, thus violating the prohibition against doing any work on that day. The story runs in this fashion:

Now the Israelites were in the wilderness and they found a man gathering wood on the Sabbath Day. So those who found him gathering wood brought him to Moses and to Aaron and to the whole assembly. They detained him in the guard house, because it had not been explained what should be done to him. Then Yahweh said to Moses: "The man shall surely be put to death. The whole assembly shall stone him with stones, outside the camp." So the whole assembly brought him outside the camp and they stoned him with stones and he died, as Yahweh had commanded Moses.

It will be seen that the story is very much like the one previously cited from Leviticus (24:10–16). In both cases, a violation of one of the Ten Commandments is recorded, and the man responsible is arrested pending sentence and the imposition of appropriate punishment. Similarly, in both cases the determination of the penalty (death by stoning by the whole assembly) is made by Yahweh through direct communication with Moses. The action by God is taken to supplement the Decalogue itself, which only lists the injunctions but in no instance specifies the punishments. The severity of the penalty serves to emphasize the centrality and essentiality of these terms of the covenant.[10] Anything less than the removal of the offender could and would implicate the whole community in the offense and ultimately lead to abrogation of the compact and the dissolution of the nation. The requirement that the whole adult community participate in the act of judgment symbolizes the deliberate and emphatic dissociation of the group from the violator and his violation, and shows the community's willing acceptance of the role of agent and instrument in carrying out the judgment of God. While such an action (gathering wood on the

Sabbath) might seem to us a minor infraction deserving no more than a warning or a fine, it is treated with the utmost seriousness as a challenge to the authority of God. Prophets and priests throughout the biblical period (e.g., Amos 8:5; Isaiah 56:2–6, 58:13–14; Jeremiah 17:21–27) make the issue of Sabbath observance central and critical for the survival of the community; the violation of the sanctity of the Sabbath through mundane labor is regarded as a major cause of the collapse of the nation.

I shall have something more to say about the smaller groupings of the commandments later on, but now we must turn to the fifth book (Deuteronomy) and the fifth commandment, which reads as follows:

> Honor your father and mother, so that your days may be prolonged in the land that Yahweh your God is going to give you. (Exodus 20:12)

Once again there is a brief account of a violation of this commandment in the fifth book, the Book of Deuteronomy, only it is couched in the hypothetical terminology of case law: prescribing the punishment for a specified crime. In other words, the formulation in Deuteronomy is a stage beyond that reached in Leviticus and Numbers, and we might look at the similar commandment in Exodus 21:17 ("Whoever curses his father or mother shall be put to death") as a type of intermediate point in the process. In the earlier books, we are given the incident or episode that provided the basis or precedent on which the punishment for the particular violation was set down. Here we have the more general formulation, presumably derived from a particular incident, now lost, or no longer included in the biblical tradition.

The case is stated in the following manner, and shows how violations of the fifth commandment were to be handled:

> If a man has a son who is contumacious and rebellious (i.e., stubbornly rebellious) and will not obey the orders of his father or his mother; and if they chastise (discipline)

him and he persists in his disobedience, then his father and his mother shall lay hold of him and bring him forth to the elders of his city and to the gate of his place. And they (the parents) shall say to the elders of his city: This son of ours is contumacious and rebellious, and he will not obey our orders; he is (also) an idler and a sot. Then all the men of his city shall stone him with stones until he is dead. So shall you destroy the evil from your midst. And as for all Israel, let them pay heed and show reverence. (Deuteronomy 21: 18–21)

While we do not have an actual instance of parental abuse, the case offered here can serve as an adequate substitute, if we recognize that many such cases were not merely hypothetical, but were formulations and generalizations based on actual experience. We may be certain that this law, like the others, addressed real-life circumstances and hence reflected the same sort of actuality described in the preceding examples. It is simply another way of transposing the Decalogue from oracular terms of the heavenly covenant made between God and Israel to the earthly arena in which human beings live. We should also recognize the limitations imposed on our editor by the nature of the materials available in the books under consideration: Leviticus, Numbers, and Deuteronomy. They are books dominated by priestly considerations and concerns, and they are not rich in stories, which might serve better or more colorfully to illustrate covenantal violations. We can also see a difference in approach and resolution between the P(riestly)-Writer in Leviticus and Numbers and the D(euteronomistic)-Writer in Deuteronomy. But the editor of the whole must take what is at hand and make the best of it.

We turn now to the second half of the Decalogue and will deal in order with commandments six through nine, noting again that we expect to run out of books of the Primary History (or Enneateuch) before we run out of commandments. Before proceeding, however, we must comment about the order of the next three commandments, numbers six through eight, which are noteworthy for their extreme brevity: they each consist of only two words in the Hebrew—the negative particle plus the verb form (which contains both pronoun subject and verbal action). The order of these in Exodus 20 (and Deuteronomy 5) is as follows:

6. *lō' tirṣāḥ*—You shall not kill.
7. *lō' tin'āp*—You shall not commit adultery.
8. *lō' tignōb*—You shall not steal.

We will look for significant violations of these commandments in the stories of Joshua, Judges, and 1 and 2 Samuel; we will find violations, but not in the same order. Obviously the editor will not have much choice in the matter, since he can hardly rearrange the books of the Former Prophets or alter their sequence; they are clearly intended to be in chronological order and cannot be shuffled around. But the editor, being a resourceful person, and familiar with other traditions concerning the order of these three commandments, could appeal to such diversity to justify his own rearrangement. In the current case the order will be as follows:

8. Theft
6. Murder
7. Adultery

It may be pointed out that in the Septuagint, the order of the passage in Exodus 20 is as follows:

7. Adultery
8. Theft
6. Murder

In other sources, including the Nash Papyrus, Philo, and the New Testament (Luke 18:20, Romans 13:9, and James 2:11),[11] the order is:

7. Adultery
6. Murder
8. Theft

While these cases indicate that alternate orders existed, they do not support the arrangement our editor requires and that we propose. For that we appeal to an abbreviated version of the Decalogue offered by Jeremiah in his well-known Sermon in the Temple courtyard (Jeremiah 7: 8–11). In verse 9 the order is:

8. Stealing
6. Murder
7. Adultery

This is the order in which the commandments are violated in Joshua, Judges, and Samuel (Hosea 4:2 attests to yet another order: murder, stealing, and adultery). There may even be a connection, since we are aware of a resemblance and a possible relationship between the Book of Jeremiah and the Deuteronomistic History (including the books from Deuteronomy through Kings—the major component in length of the Primary History; see lecture 2, pp. 46–47). So far as the prose sections of Jeremiah are concerned, there is a similarity of style, as well as a sharing of themes and motifs, that strongly supports the idea of connection and relationship: so much so that a link between these works can be found in the person of Baruch ben-Neriah. This is the scribe who was responsible for at least two versions of the Book of Jeremiah and who may well have had an important role in the compilation and production of the great Deuteronomistic History.[12] Be that as it may, the compiler of this work wished to include in the story of the decline and fall of the Israelite commonwealth illustrative and dramatic examples of the violation of individual commandments that involved important people and jeopardized the whole community while affecting the course of the nation's history.

We can now turn to the sixth book, the Book of Joshua. As it turns out, the major crime, or transgression of the covenant, is a case of theft. This is a violation of the eighth commandment in the conventional ordering (Exodus 20 and Deuteronomy 5), but, as noted, corresponds to our number six following the list in Jeremiah 7. The story is given in great detail in Joshua 7: it is that of Achan ben-Carmi of the tribe of Judah. In the opening verse (7:1), the writer lists the essential components and focuses attention on Achan and his criminal behavior in stealing from the booty that was seized in the capture of Jericho and set aside as sacred to Yahweh:

> The Israelites committed a grave offense regarding the dedicated booty. Achan, the son of Carmi, the son of Zabdi, the son of Zerach of the tribe of Judah, took some of the sacred booty, and the wrath of Yahweh was kindled against the Israelites. (Joshua 7:1)

While space restrictions do not permit us to deal with the story in detail, certain points need to be made.

First, the gravity of the situation is illustrated by the account (verses 2–5) of Israel's defeat at the hands of the men of Ai, which jeopardizes their foothold on the West Bank and threatens the whole settlement in the land of Canaan.

Second, the punishment meted out to Achan (verses 25–26) is even more severe and extensive than in the previous cases. Achan is executed by stoning, with the whole community participating, and his children are executed with him (Hebrew *kārēt*, literally "cut off"). Thus the whole family was wiped out for the violation of the covenant, carrying out the threat made in the Decalogue (Exodus 20:5; Deuteronomy 5:9) about visiting the punishment for violations of the covenant on the descendants of the violator (as well as on him). In the Decalogue, this type of punishment is attached directly to the first two commandments (dealing with apostasy and idolatry), but it could be applied, as we see here, to other violations as well.

Third, the story shows how the crime of theft was construed

as a capital offense on a par with the other commandments, and punishable in the same manner (by community stoning). While the commandment itself, like the immediately associated ones (six through nine), has its primary and general application to human situations (as also spelled out in the tenth and last commandment), the act here has centered attention on a singular example of theft, one that involves the taking of valuable items from the divine treasury, the booty dedicated to the God who brought victory at Jericho. In most cases, theft would not be considered a capital offense; the wrongdoer would be punished by a fine, the imposition of damages (requiring payment of double the amount or a larger multiple), or in some other suitable fashion. Such cases would hardly serve the stipulated purpose, but the extraordinary case of Achan does so admirably and thus fits the pattern and the scheme we have outlined. Stealing from the sacred treasure is equivalent to the other major offenses against the deity described in the other commandments: apostasy, idolatry, blasphemy, and Sabbath-breaking. It thus merits the same punishment. The treatment of the event is much the same, with God taking a direct hand in exposing the crime and the criminal and in imposing the penalty, thus creating a precedent for future similar breaches and defining for all time the nature and gravity of the offense. The editor/compiler has adapted the commandment and structured the story in order to fit the overall pattern and so emphasize the importance of the commandments and the threat to the life of the community; the story is also structured to show both the divine provision for dealing with violations, and the nation's narrow escape from the consequences of divine wrath. As with the other instances of violation, the example chosen by the compiler for this commandment is not intended to exhaust the range of meanings for the commandment.

When we come to the seventh book, Judges, we will look for a story illustrating the seventh commandment, which in our revised numbering—and as ordered in Jeremiah 7—will be the prohibition of murder, or more generally homicide or manslaying. Inevitably, there are many cases of such killing, beginning with Cain's murder of Abel (Genesis 4) and proceeding through the Bible to the murder of the righteous priest, Zechariah, at the behest of King Joash (2 Chronicles 24: 20–22, which also records the subsequent death of Joash by assassination; cf. Matthew 23:34–36 and Luke 11:49–51). Nevertheless, one such case stands out in the annals of Israel and is described in such a way as to link this murder with the Decalogue and also to jeopardize the existence of the community. The presentation of the episode is similar to that in the story in Joshua and to other pairs of violation stories— e.g., commandments 3 and 4 in Leviticus and Numbers (cf. the combination of 1 and 2 in Exodus), and also in the pairing of 8 and 9 in Samuel and Kings.

Although the Book of Judges records a number of killings, e.g., Eglon by Ehud, Sisera by Jael, and numerous Philistines by Samson, none of these qualifies for our purposes, because not only are they not considered violations of the commandment, but are regarded as righteous deeds for the sake of the community. The story we have in mind comes at the very end of the Book of Judges, is spelled out in great detail over three chapters, and fully qualifies according to our criteria. While the case in question (Judges 19–21) depicts a mass rape and abuse of the victim (the Levite's concubine), the woman is described in the story as "the murdered woman" (Hebrew hā'iššâ hannirṣāḥâ, Judges 20:4). The verbal root is the same as the one used in the Decalogue: rṣḥ. Furthermore, the crime is described by the author/editor as the worst in the history of the commonwealth, since its inception up to that time:

There has not happened, nor has there been seen anything like this since the day that the Israelites went up from the land of Egypt until this day. (Judges 19:30)

Not only was the crime a brutal and appalling one by any standards, contemporary or subsequent, but it was compounded by the Benjaminites who refused to cooperate with the other tribes in the investigation and resolution of the matter. In the end there was open civil war, the near-destruction of one whole tribe (Benjamin), and the near-dissolution of the entire league. Once again, however, Israel was spared through divine guidance and the timely intervention of devoted and dedicated men.

Nevertheless, the countdown goes on, and the time clock continues to run. We have now reached the eighth book of the Hebrew Canon, the Book of Samuel.[13] It should be observed that originally, and in the official Hebrew Canon, Samuel consisted of a single long book, which was subsequently divided into two parts, presumably for ease in handling and for reference purposes. The same is true, incidentally, of two other books in the Hebrew Bible, Kings and Chronicles. It is no accident that these are the three longest books (by word count) in the Hebrew Bible (between 24,000 and 26,000 words) and are therefore the most likely to be divided. The division may have occurred when the Greek translation of these books was made, since the translations are longer than the originals and we can speculate that the book had reached the practical limit in terms of scroll length. Thus anything longer than that would have been divided. In any case, the eighth book is Samuel, and in our count the eighth commandment will be the prohibition against adultery.

While the latter is often mentioned in the Hebrew Bible and especially in the Latter Prophets, there is, in fact, only one particular example of this crime spelled out in detail in the Bible with names of persons and places and specific occasions or actions. It is the well-known case of David the king, who took Bathsheba, the wife of Uriah the Hittite, and subsequently had Uriah killed in battle to conceal the original crime. The story receives a great deal of attention (2 Samuel 11–12). It is referred to elsewhere in the Book of Samuel, not only because the king was involved, but because of the significant effects and consequences for the kingdom and the dynasty. The climax is the confrontation between the angry prophet Nathan and the guilty but ultimately repentant King David. Without going into either details or ramifications, we can point out that for the author/editor, the adultery with Bathsheba was a turning point in the reign of David and for the history of the kingdom. All the subsequent trials and ills of his later years, the

31

rebellions and machinations, are described as stemming from that violation by the king—who compounded adultery with murder, forfeited the respect and loyalty of his troops, and thus distanced himself from his God and the covenant given him, and also from the privileged status he had enjoyed as the anointed of Yahweh. The peril for the country is amply documented, as well as the act of divine remission and compassion. Once again, the kingdom escaped its fate, and the dynasty was preserved for the sake of the nation.

For the ninth commandment and its violation we turn to the Book of Kings (1 Kings 21). The House of Ahab and Jezebel was not as fortunate as that of David, although the case of covenant and commandment violation recorded in the ninth book (Kings) is parallel to the earlier account in many respects: once again, royalty is involved and the action produces widespread and very serious consequences for the kingdom. In this story, the ninth commandment is involved, and once again the case is spelled out in considerable detail. The commandment deals with false testimony in a legal proceeding, what might (loosely) be called perjury today. The main difference is that in our courts practically all the participants are under oath or solemn affirmation, whereas in ancient Israel, oaths were invoked only under special conditions and only on the witnesses. The case recorded in 1 Kings 21 is the well-known episode involving Naboth and his vineyard. In the story, the king and queen engage in the procurement of false testimony against Naboth so as to deprive him (and his family) of life and property and thereby to acquire the coveted vineyard for themselves. It is not only a blatant violation of the ninth commandment, but the felony is compounded by the total abuse of the judicial system, which is used to commit a terrible crime rather than to correct injustice and restore equity.

Once again we have an angry prophet of Yahweh, in this case Elijah, who denounces the guilty parties and decrees dire punishment for this deliberate and wanton act. Once again the king is faced with the undeniable facts and is remorseful and repentant.

And again the deity is merciful and postpones the evil day of judgment and the final historical settling of accounts that is not long in coming, especially in terms of what remains to be told. We are at the midpoint in the book of Kings, and before it is concluded, both Israel and Judah will have come to violent ends as nations—their armies defeated, their countries conquered, their capital cities destroyed, and their leading citizens taken into captivity.

The Naboth episode is placed by the compiler near the end of the Primary History, although not necessarily near the end in historical terms. The implication is that, after these events, not only is the house of Omri/Ahab finished, but Israel itself is facing a terminus. In the near-term a bloody revolution, led by Elisha and Jehu, saved the day for Israel, and the nation lasted another 100 years or so. But its doom was sealed, and in the end it was destroyed for its violation of the covenant, as illustrated by the transgressions against the Decalogue.

The Southern Kingdom, Judah, lasted longer, but it was on notice, too. The string had run out, and in God's own time the end would come as it did about 135 years after the fall of the Northern Kingdom.

We have come to the end of our string as well: nine books, nine commandments. Before proceeding to summary and summation, we need to say something about the tenth commandment. Since there are or could be only nine books, some device or mechanism is required to handle the tenth commandment. We may look at the situation in two ways, both of which can claim validity.

In the first, Israel (and Judah) teeter on the edge of oblivion. That means that they have run out of most of their chances, but since this is biblical history and not Greek tragedy, their nemesis will be of their own making. They hold the key to their fate and the chances remain open. So there is always one more chance.

The second way is to recognize both the distinctive nature of the tenth commandment and also its role as an element or ingredient in several of the episodes already discussed. In this respect it serves as a motivation clause underlying the commission of crimes spelled out elsewhere in the commandments or the regulations of the Torah.

The commandment reads as follows:

> You shall not desire (or covet) your neighbor's house. You shall not desire your neighbor's wife, his man- or maid-servant, his ox or his ass, or anything at all that belongs to your neighbor. (Exodus 20:17)

The version in Deuteronomy 5 (verse 21) differs slightly but significantly in exchanging wife for house, thus placing the wife first and the house and its retainers second. In addition, a different but synonymous verb is used for the second clause in Deuteronomy:[14]

Exodus 20	Deuteronomy 5
lō' taḥmōd	*wĕlō' taḥmod*
("You shall not desire")	("and you shall not desire")
lō'-taḥmōd	*wĕlō' tit'awweh*
("You shall not desire")	("and you shall not long for")

There is also the question of whether the statements consist of one or two commandments. The prevailing scholarly view is that a single commandment is involved and that the second clause elaborates on the basic theme, so that the two statements together offer a comprehensive picture of the force and extent of the commandment.

Two additional points may be made. The emphasis in this commandment is on motivation or attitude, rather than action, as is clearly the case with the other commandments. It functions therefore as a complement or supplement to several of the latter commandments (especially the last five), providing the motivation clause or explanation of the mental or emotional process behind the commission of the crime.

It is not surprising that there is no specific or particular example of the violation of the tenth commandment or the imposition of a penalty for such a violation. In short, in biblical law as in Common Law (English and American) and the law of most civilized countries, attitude or internal feelings do not constitute a punishable offense. Only when these feelings are attached to an illicit action do they figure in criminal proceedings. Coveting or desiring what belongs to another is undoubtedly a sin against the will of God according to the Bible, but such a sinful desire only becomes a punishable crime when conjoined with the actual commission of the offense. Thus, in the series we have been considering, especially the sixth through the ninth commandments, what lay behind the crime in each case was the illicit desire, the sinful urge to take what belonged to another: the booty from Jericho in the case of Achan, who confesses that he saw the various items in the spoil and "I desired them" (Hebrew ḥmd, the same verb used in the Decalogue). When he coveted the sacred booty, he sinned against God and violated the tenth commandment, but only when he seized the booty did he commit a legally punishable crime. The same can be said of the criminals in the story of Judges, whose illegal desire for the Levite led ultimately to the commission of the crime of murder against his companion. In the case of David and Bathsheba, it was David's lust after the wife of another man that led to the act of adultery. In the Sermon on the Mount, Jesus in a well-known pronouncement (Matthew 5:27–28) explains that such lust is equivalent to adultery, i.e., the motivation makes one guilty in the eyes of God. In this way, Jesus effectively removes the rules of the Kingdom from the area of jurisprudence and returns them to the realm of inner commitment and dedication to the will of the deity, which was also the original focus and locus of the Decalogue (note again the absence of specific sanctions and punishments). In legal terms, therefore, David sins against God and violates the tenth commandment by desiring to possess the wife of Uriah, but he commits adultery only when the sexual act is consummated.

Likewise, in the case of Naboth's Vineyard, it was the desire of the king for this property that violated the tenth commandment. However, the crime specified in the ninth commandment was the legally punishable offense, suborning witnesses to give false testimony against Naboth so that the king could acquire the property adjoining the royal palace in Jezreel.

We can see, therefore, how the tenth commandment interacts with the others, supplies the underlying motivation clause, and thus has been violated throughout the history of the covenant between God and Israel. At the same time, no specific case involving only coveting (without corresponding and consequent action) is described as with the others. We can repeat what was said earlier, that the tenth commandment is different from the others in not being a punishable offense by itself but in being an important component of the other crimes illustrated and described in the foregoing books, especially regarding commandments six through nine.

We have, therefore, come full circle. We have completed the list of the ten commandments and we have covered the nine books of the Primary History. We have shown that with a modicum of ingenuity and adjustment we can correlate the two groups, the Decalogue and the Primary History, and make a dramatically effective correspondence between the two—namely a one-for-one correspondence between commandments and books leading to a climax or culmination in the final collapse of the two kingdoms, the end of national history, and the Babylonian Captivity.

Now we must make an effort to offer a rational explanation of how such a correlation came about in view of the heterogeneous character of the Primary History and its clearly multiple authorship. Between the extremes of sheer coincidence (buttressed by the ingenuity of a modern analyst looking for such correlations) on the one hand, and unitary authorship (or in this case a creative editor who deliberately sets out to construct a history of his people on the framework of the Decalogue) on the other, we adopt a mediating position. Such a position recognizes the heterogeneous character of the book and its multiple objectives and purposes, but it also affirms the deliberate editing by one or more persons to achieve and preserve an overall unity by the strategic highlighting of particular themes and devices to bring out the central story: the covenant between God and Israel, the ultimate consequences of the relationship, and the judgment on and verdict against the nation-states.

We may begin with the Deuteronomic History, the identity and scope of which are generally recognized by scholars.[15] This work, extending from Deuteronomy through Kings, clearly contains many of the essential ingredients for our hypothesis. The author/editor has set up the history of Israel in the light of the covenant at Horeb (Sinai), and has begun his narrative with the recapitulation of the Decalogue (Deuteronomy 5 after the introduction, chaps. 1–4). For this editor, the Decalogue is the focus of attention from the beginning of the story, and there can be little doubt that he has structured the narrative around the theme of Israel's struggle to fulfill its obligation to God under the terms of the covenant and how it finally failed. There can be little doubt, as well, that the great, colorful, and dramatic episodes found in the successive books of this work—Joshua, Judges, Samuel, Kings—were chosen to illustrate violations of the commandments and the dire consequences threatened as a result. For reasons already explained, the compiler has followed, in the narrative, an order of the commandments different from the order established in the Decalogue. In addition, he has concentrated attention on the second panel of the laws (numbers six through ten) rather than the entire Decalogue. Nevertheless, the editor leads off with the initial double violation at Mount Horeb (or Sinai) and continues to stress the central and dominant importance of the initial commandment(s) throughout the narrative. So all the essential elements of our reconstruction were already present in the Deuteronomic work, including the central theme of covenant violation and punishment, as well as extended narratives illustrating dramatic violations of the specific commandments, especially the last five (corresponding generally and not unintentionally to the five books in this work).

When the D-Work was combined with the P-Work in the sixth century, the editor already had the general structure of the D-Work, as well as the other tradition (the P-Work), to build on and needed only to join the two works to produce the complete pattern we have observed. There are differences in approach and treatment of the two groups of commandments, as we have shown in the preceding pages, but there is also a coalescence or confluence of purposes and goals, so that the end product reads in a smooth unitary narrative from first to last but does not conceal the seams by which the two works are joined. The P-Work also began its narrative of the Mosaic covenant with the Sinai episodes, and in the succeeding books, from Exodus through Numbers, it shows how the commandments and their violations correspond to the books. There is a major difference in the treatment of these themes between the two works: in the D-Work the episodes are central, dominant, and decisive for the history of the nation, while in the P-Work the episodes are provided to illustrate the correlation of the commandments to the life of the nation, and how, through violation, the necessary legislation was enacted to make the breaking of the rules capital offenses. The one exception involves the episode of the Golden Calf and the first two commandments, the only instance in which there is extensive duplication and overlapping between the P- and D-Works. Just as the repetition of the Decalogue emphasizes its importance for the story, so the recollection of the episode of the Golden Calf in Deuteronomy underscores its centrality in the tradition.

All that the final editor had to do was to connect the two works at the appropriate point (attaching D to P at the end of Numbers and at the beginning of Deuteronomy) and to make sure that the violations expressed as early as the Book of Exodus (chap. 32) were then recapitulated and resumed in Deuteronomy (chap. 5 and following). The remaining items were already in place.

We should not misconstrue the phenomenon described above. The fact that the particular device and pattern have not been widely observed in the past should caution us against supposing that it was the major or central consideration of the authors or compilers when they set about their work. It was simply another, if dramatic, way of showing and stressing the central theme of the history of Israel, another way of illustrating or reflecting the unity of the account comprising the nine books of the Primary History.

To summarize: the purpose of the author/editor was to show how God created Israel to be his people and then formally sealed the relationship through a covenant that was concluded between them at Sinai/Horeb, mediated by Moses, and summarized or epitomized in the Decalogue. Israel's subsequent history could be told in terms of its successive violations of the commandments—one by one, book by book, until Israel ran out of options and possibilities and was destroyed as a nation, and its people taken into captivity.

The Latter Prophets

The section of the Hebrew Bible called the Former Prophets constitutes, on the one hand, a continuation of the Torah (the first part), forming the Primary History (from Genesis through Kings), and on the other, an important link with the second section of the Prophets, the so-called Latter Prophets. The Latter Prophets, consisting of four books (originally scrolls), match the Former Prophets in number and length (four books totaling about 70,000 words for each group). The organization and arrangement of these books were deliberate, reflecting a common or single purpose, and they were managed by a single person or small committee.

The relationship of the Latter Prophets to the Primary History, or more specifically to the Former Prophets, can be described in the following way. The countdown of the Ten Commandments described in the first lecture brings us to the halfway point in the Book of Kings (just one chapter from the end of 1 Kings, which, however, is almost 1,000 words longer than 2 Kings); at this point the story is almost complete, leaving somewhat less than 10 percent of the narrative yet to be told. Nevertheless, the period remaining covers more than 250 years. So the narrative moves quite rapidly and laconically from this point on. In fact, the first half of

2 Kings is taken up with the violent rebellion generated by Elijah and Elisha, the prophets who led the opposition to the House of Omri (and Ahab), which was carried out by the general of the armies, Jehu. The latter put an end to the dynasty of Omri and Ahab and made himself king instead. It is not until the reign of the third successor of Jehu, his great-grandson Jeroboam (II), that the Latter Prophets come into the picture (2 Kings 14ff.) early in the eighth century B.C.E. Only a quarter of the ninth and last book of the Primary History remains when the juncture with the Latter Prophets is reached, although almost two centuries of Israelite and Judahite history remain to be covered.

The linkage is important for understanding both works. It is clear that the Latter Prophets were included as a supplement to the Primary History and that the two were intended to be read together. The Latter Prophets provide extended additional details to the rather brief and terse account preserved in the Primary History, as though the editor wished the reader to turn to the more expanded work for additional important and necessary information. The Latter Prophets continue on past the close of the Primary History, from the Babylonian into the Persian period. The Primary History ends around 560 B.C.E., while the last date attested in the Latter Prophets (in Zechariah 7) is the fourth year of Darius I of Persia, ca. 518 B.C.E. The great bulk of the material in the Latter Prophets coincides and overlaps with the closing portion of the Primary History. Thus the entire books of Jeremiah and Ezekiel belong to the period of the Primary History; in fact the last chapter of Jeremiah is almost a duplicate of the last chapter of 2 Kings—showing, in my opinion, that the same person was responsible for the production and publication of the Book of Jeremiah and the Primary History. In these chapters (2 Kings 25 and Jeremiah 52) is found the critically important final date of both books, which employs a formula unique to those books but which corresponds to the usage in the Book of Ezekiel only. The point is that the date is calculated according to what would have been the regnal years of the exiled king, Jehoiachin (as followed by Ezekiel, who lived in Babylon where that king also resided), whereas in

Kings and Jeremiah dates are reckoned according to the reign of the incumbent king, Zedekiah, at least while that king ruled in Jerusalem. In addition, 1 Isaiah (through chap. 39 but omitting chapters 34–35, which belong to 2 Isaiah) and most of the book of the Twelve Minor Prophets also belong to the period included in the Primary History, excluding with relative certainty only the last three books of the twelve (Haggai, Zechariah, Malachi—the first two of these are explicitly dated in the reign of Darius, while from Zechariah 9–14 and through Malachi there are no precise dates, leaving open the question of their period and provenience).[1]

It can be seen, then, that the Latter Prophets lock into place toward the end of the Primary History (i.e., Former Prophets), and greatly expand and elaborate on the last part of 2 Kings—adding perhaps 60,000 words to the material in 2 Kings, which for chapters 14–25 might be only about 6,000 words. In addition, there is a supplement or epilogue, which brings the story down to the time of Darius I of Persia, in whose reign (522–486 B.C.E.) an event of momentous importance for the community of Judah took place: the restoration and rededication of the Temple in Jerusalem. Just this brief and extremely dry summary of contents suffices to illustrate and illuminate the paradox or anomaly about the Latter Prophets that I wish to discuss.

While the bulk of the Latter Prophets deals with the same material as the Primary History (especially at the end) and for the most part only paints in more colorful and extensive detail the disaster that came to the land and its people—repeating over and over again the data of destruction and exile, of affliction and oppression—nevertheless, the intent and objective of this collection of prophetic oracles and narratives are clearly to present a different or contrary picture of events, and especially of divine purposes and ends. From first to last, but especially last, the end of the process is seen to be the restoration of the commonwealth, the renewal of the people, and the rebuilding of the land, its cities, and, above all, the Temple. While the distribution of the content may give greater weight to defeat, disaster, and destruction, the contrast is made all the more striking by the colorful description and poetic eloquence of those who depict the glorious future of the land and people—already in the initial stages of realization. We shall point to certain images in the Major Prophets (i.e., Isaiah, Jeremiah, and Ezekiel) that exemplify this thesis.

The most striking and vivid image of all is to be found in the thirty-seventh chapter of the Book of Ezekiel, which captures the essence of the prophetic perspective on the historic experience of Israel (and Judah). In a single indelible picture it presents the demise of the nation and incorporates the rhetorical question posed to the prophet:

Son of Man, can these bones live?

The vision, no doubt stimulated by the battle-strewn dead after the Babylonian invasion, conveys both a message of judgment and doom fulfilled in the recent military defeats and political disasters, and through the query, the assurance of hope for the future in a national resurrection. Ezekiel comes at the turning point of the history of the people of God: the death of the nation and the beginning of its revival. What led up to and away from that central and all-encompassing disaster? Out of death, deserved and inevitable, would come life, undeserved but irreversibly ordained by the same God who had meted out death to his own people. Yahweh, the God of Israel, who had destroyed his people, must restore them if only to provide meaning and substance to his name. The God of Israel must have an Israel of which to be God, so that his full real name will be honored among all the nations: Yahweh of Hosts, the God of Israel. Ezekiel, along with Jeremiah, is above all the prophet of the transition—from death to life, or real national demise to genuine renewal and restoration.

For Jeremiah, there are many vivid and dramatic moments or occasions. We see him passionately denouncing all those in authority in Judah; then, when disaster struck and the leadership was gone (removed by death or exile), we see him pleading just as passionately with new leaders to remain with the rubble of their cities and the ruins of their lands—to stay and "tough it out" because God, their God, the same God who brought about their total ruination and devastation had repented yet again, this time concerning the destruction of the holy city itself. God was now determined to salvage his people and his community, and he would establish them once more in their land. The prophet was notably unsuccessful in persuading his countrymen to listen to the word of God, whether in warning and threat or in comfort and promise. But among the quieter moments in a tension-filled, violence-threatening career, we note a commercial transaction: the purchase by the prophet of a small piece of land (as shown by the price of seventeen shekels), in his homeland of Benjamin (Jeremiah 32). Without delving into the details of the real-estate deal, we note that it involved a suddenly destitute relative who may have been concerned about getting cash for a piece of property that was losing value almost daily as the advancing Babylonian army and its allies overran and occupied the areas around Jerusalem, where this property was located. To put it mildly, investment by Israelites in such property was contraindicated. Yet despite his awareness of the patent folly of such a move, Jeremiah not only paid out the full amount—a gesture somewhat reminiscent of his ancient ancestor Abraham, who bought a tract from the Hittites in Hebron as a burial place for his wife and himself—but recorded the transaction and the deed with great care and through the good offices of his scribal companion Baruch, so that it would serve as a symbol and send a message across the years and the distances. By his purchase, he was buying a stake in the future commonwealth of Israel, which though defeated and driven out, would one day return to claim possession of its land.

As already indicated, the Latter Prophets are linked to the two great historical works in the Hebrew Bible: the Primary History and the Chronicler's Work. We can proceed to spell out these relationships more specifically and more in detail.

First, it is generally agreed that the Primary History consists of two major and originally independent works (as discussed in our previous lecture): the P-Work (essentially covering Genesis through Numbers) and the D-Work (from Deuteronomy through

Kings).[2] While both incorporate older sources and are not themselves entirely unified and coherent literary works, they reflect and express major editorial activity in the First Temple period. Both relative and absolute chronology for these two works is still much debated, and our own opinion that they are roughly contemporaneous seventh-century B.C.E. compilations (perhaps a little earlier for one and a little later for the other, or vice versa) has not gained widespread acceptance. For our purposes, however, it is not necessary to resolve the issue.[3] Although we are primarily interested in the connections between these works and the several major and minor prophets, we would affirm and argue for the combination of these substantial literary products into the single Primary History during the exile in the first half of the sixth century B.C.E. While they are very distinctive with respect to language, usage, and style (for the most part the separation of P from D is easily accomplished and generally agreed to by all serious scholars), along with special interests and emphases, it is not necessary, however, to assume or posit that originally the P-Work must have ended abruptly at the end of Numbers (and in the classic analysis much of Joshua was included as part of the P-Work) or that the D-Work commenced only with Deuteronomy—although a stronger case can be made for the second premise.

What concerns us here, however, is the association of each of these constituent parts of the Primary History with major prophetic books. The similarities between Jeremiah (in its present form) and the D-Work, on the one hand, and between Ezekiel and the P-Work on the other, have long been noted.[4] Without trying to resolve disputed points as to the real relationship between the prophets and the associated works, we can acknowledge that there are inevitable tensions between prophets and priests (even if in both cases the prophets are themselves priests and presumably members of the groups involved in the production of the larger works). It is probably correct to distinguish the central message of the prophets from the narrative or descriptive accounts in their own books and in the associated larger literature. What we wish to emphasize is the literary connection (regardless of dependence, direction, or relative chronology) and to suggest that each of these major prophets was claimed by the related group as authority and spokesman for that group and its literature. I suggest that it was deemed both necessary and valuable to enlist or co-opt a major prophet in connection with the production and promulgation of an authoritative work. Naturally, the original and ultimate human authority for both groups and works is Moses, the man of God and the model for prophets and prophecy. In addition, however, a contemporary messenger of God would be claimed as well, the modern representative of the movement and the spiritual heir of Moses himself. We can even make some suggestions about the nature or character of the association.

In the case of Jeremiah, we have information about the composition and compilation of his book, especially regarding the prominent role of Baruch the Scribe. While I do not agree with the recent suggestion that Jeremiah himself had anything to do with the D-Work (Deuteronomic History), I think it is quite likely that Baruch did, and that he was one of a very small group of Deuteronomists responsible for the D-Work.[5] The fact that both the D-Work (and the Primary History) and the Book of Jeremiah end with the same chapter (2 Kings 25 = Jeremiah 52) shows that the final editor wished to link the two works. In my judgment this editor brought out both of them at the same time, namely in or around 562/1 B.C.E. In a similar way, we can connect Ezekiel with the P-Work and Priestly Group, although we lack specific information about the way in which they may have worked together (or at odds). Clearly Ezekiel and P are different, if only because they differ so markedly about prescriptions for the Temple (Tabernacle in P) and about many other matters of priestly concern. In spite of that, Ezekiel was present in Babylon with the exiled high priestly family (of whom he clearly approved, at least in principle and by lineage), and no doubt his was a dominant voice in the preparation and production of the major biblical works already described: the Primary History and the exilic Prophetic Corpus (which will be discussed later). In both cases—Jeremiah and the D-Work and Ezekiel and the P-Work—the evidence is primarily and persuasively linguistic and literary. We would argue further that when the two works were combined late in the exile, a compromise was reached between the two groups, namely the D-people presumably based in Egypt and the P-people based in Babylon.[6] As a result, not only was the bulk of each of the works preserved (with whatever differences, inconsistencies, and anomalies contained in them), but both prophets were included as well. There were also, however, considerable and substantial differences between them, not only in details (such as the contrast between the forty-year prophecy of Ezekiel about the length of the exile and the seventy-year prophecy of Jeremiah about the hegemony of the Neo-Babylonian Empire), but also in matters of central importance. Nevertheless, it was believed that they agreed about the judgment of God against his people and his city and temple, and also about the ultimate return and restoration.

Second, when it comes to the Chronicler's Work, we believe that a case can be made for the association between it and the Book of Isaiah. The situation is somewhat more complex, and we are mindful that neither work is unified but rather both are composites. Nevertheless, the two major points of contact coincide with the major editorial seams in both works. Taking both works in their present forms, we can point to the fact that both are postexilic in date, and both make much of the return from exile in the reign of Cyrus the Great. While I believe that the event itself is still in the future in the so-called Second Isaiah (chaps. 40–55), it is clearly expected, and the role of Cyrus is very important (see chaps. 44–45) in terms of what he has accomplished and of what is yet to come. Similarly, in the Chronicler's Work (hereafter C-Work) the Edict of Cyrus is the pivot on which the two main sections turn: thus Chronicles ends with the Edict of Cyrus (2 Chronicles 36:22–23) and Ezra-Nehemiah begins with it (Ezra 1:1–4). These are the only two works in the Hebrew Bible that speak of Cyrus at all (apart from Daniel, which does not enter into consideration for various reasons), and they share a common outlook about him and the future of Israel (or rather Judah). Of course, this is only part of the story, since both Isaiah and the C-Work deal with other matters, especially with the eighth century B.C.E. In passing, let me say that while we can hardly speak of the unity of the C-Work anymore, especially in light of recent critical work on its contents and character,[7] I believe, nevertheless, that we can continue to speak of a final compilation of Chronicles and Ezra-Nehemiah, even if we cannot and should not regard it as a single work by a single author or editor. I have suggested elsewhere[8] how I think the compilation took place over an extended period of time, and I am still inclined to believe that there was a version or versions of the Chronicler's History immediately after the exile and perhaps in pre-exilic times. I believe that Ezra may well have been the ultimate editor of the C-Work, at least of the material preceding his time, and that his memoirs were attached to that work either by him or, more likely, by someone else. In the end, I think that Nehemiah was responsible not only for his own memoirs, but that he sponsored and sanctioned the publication of the combined work. He himself wrote his own memoirs in a very distinctive style, but he was not directly involved in the production of the whole work, which was left to others. I am attracted to the suggestion (made by Baruch Halpern) that Hezekiah was the real hero of the Chronicler and that an initial work celebrated his great reform.[9] I also think that First Isaiah was associated with this reform and that the first C-Work and the first Book of Isaiah were connected in that fashion. First Isaiah, while a denunciatory prophet in the tradition of Amos (and possibly his disciple), nevertheless was remembered in tradition as the one who collaborated with the king, Hezekiah, in the salvation of Jerusalem. In its present form, therefore, First Isaiah shares with the C-Work a very positive view of Jerusalem and the Davidic dynasty, and they go together as naturally (but also in tension) as do Jeremiah and the D-Work and Ezekiel and the P-Work.

We can thus line up the Major Prophets with the major historical works of the Hebrew Bible as indicated. In the case of Isaiah, we have two prophets in all likelihood (possibly more), and we have two points of contact: First Isaiah with Hezekiah and the First Chronicler's Work, i.e., a combination made possibly in the late eighth century or early seventh century; and Second Isaiah with Cyrus and the return from exile in the late sixth century. Overall, we find numerous points of agreement in both works, especially in the emphasis on Jerusalem, the Temple, the dynasty of David, and the continuous commitment and support of Yahweh.

Third, I wish to pursue the matter of literary associations a little further and at the same time include in the overall picture the collection of Minor Prophets. First of all, I think we can link groups of Minor Prophets with Major Prophets, just as we have tried to show a significant connection between the Major Prophets and the major historical narratives in the Hebrew Bible. Thus, in the final form of the Book of the Twelve, we can recognize certain groupings with natural affinities; then, assuming some sort of intentional and underlying symmetry, we can make the rest of the assignments. Thus the last three books of the Twelve belong to the post-exilic period. Haggai and First Zechariah (chaps. 1–8) clearly do because of the dates sprinkled liberally throughout the two books, and it is generally agreed that the remainder are post-exilic as well, although opinions differ as to date and provenience.[10] I have a somewhat different theory about Zechariah 9–14 and Malachi. I think that the original collection of Minor Prophets ended with Zechariah 7–8, which give us a terminus a quo for the collection, namely in the fourth year of Darius I (the date is given in 7:1). It was compiled (at least the collection from Haggai 1 through Zechariah 8) in order to encourage the completion of the Second Temple within the time frame specified by Jeremiah (the seventy-year prediction in Jeremiah 25:11–12 and 29:10–14), as interpreted by Zechariah and possibly also Haggai, i.e., from the destruction of the First Temple until the completion of the Second Temple. According to the usual chronological reckoning, we are in the sixty-ninth or seventieth year by then, so the message is rather urgent. The actual completion and dedication took place in the sixth year of Darius I (ca. 515 B.C.E.) or slightly late by this reckoning. Then from Zechariah 9 through Malachi we have a collection of three anonymous prophecies, the dates of which range all through the period of the so-called Literary Prophets (eighth to the end of the sixth century, or possibly later). These were simply added at the end of the collection. The final edition could be as late as Ezra-Nehemiah, but there is no indication anywhere of a later date. The similarity in subject matter of some materials in Malachi and Ezra-Nehemiah suggests contemporaneity, but since there are no specific dates in the latter part of Zechariah and Malachi, it is hard to say.

Fourth, with regard to the rest of the Minor Prophets, we can assign the three eighth-century prophets to the domain of First Isaiah (already discussed in connection with the C-Work), namely Hosea, Amos, and Micah. This group balances the association of the last three (mentioned above) with Second Isaiah. While Amos, Hosea, and Micah do not occur together, they belong to the first half of the Collection of the Twelve, and there is some sense of chronological order in that book, as is recognized. In the Septuagint (the Greek translation of the Hebrew Scriptures) Hosea, Amos, and Micah are the first three, in that order. Therefore, just as the Book of Isaiah forms an envelope around Jeremiah and Ezekiel, so Hosea, Amos, and Micah form an envelope around the twelve in association with Haggai-Zechariah-Malachi (especially in the Greek version). Again we are dealing with the two ends of the prophetic era, as we have defined it. Then Jeremiah and Ezekiel would find a natural association with the remaining six prophetic books. According to its chronology, the Book of Jeremiah begins around 627 B.C.E., or when Assyria entered into its final decline and demise. The Book of Nahum belongs to this period, while Zephaniah seems to be similarly situated, although the exact provenience and date are debated. Still, it almost certainly falls within the scope of Jeremiah, which extends into the middle of the exile at least. Habakkuk likewise clearly belongs to the same era and may be even more closely associated with Jeremiah, since Habakkuk seems to speak from the perspective of one who remained in Jerusalem through the most harrowing period, as Jeremiah also did. These three books come together in the usual order and seem to belong to the same period, a period dominated by the Book of Jeremiah. We are left with three somewhat anomalous books, and their association with Ezekiel occurs more by a process of elimination than by direct connection, although the links with Ezekiel and Jeremiah can be defended. I think that we can connect Obadiah with the period of the exile, and more directly with Jeremiah than with Ezekiel. In either case, however, the period is the same, as is the point of view, since both Ezekiel and Jeremiah denounce Edom in no uncertain terms (cf. also Psalm 137 from the same period, and the Book of Lamentations). The date of Joel is problematical, and perhaps it is best left unassigned except in broad terms. The common opinion about Jonah is that it is late- or at least post-exilic, and that may be true.[11] The book's association with Assyria in its heyday would place it in the eighth century, but that is only with regard to the historical prophet and his actual circumstances. Some such reasoning may explain the placement of these books in the first half of the Twelve Prophets, but the prevailing scholarly opinion assigns these books to a later period.

We have said something about the final collection, when it was compiled, and what function and purpose it served. We have also mentioned the connections with other parts of the Hebrew Bible, mainly the large narrative units, because the prophets were historical individuals. Although only a few of them are even mentioned in the narratives,[12] they played a significant role in the period in which they lived and delivered their oracles. Now we wish to trace the precedent history of the collection that we have, and suggest that earlier collections were made that formed the nucleus of the larger expanded collection we have at present. The first collection was made in the eighth century and included, in my opinion, the four eighth-century prophets: First Isaiah, Amos, Hosea, and Micah.[13] Of these the first to be published was the Book of Amos (following the heading and its reference to the earthquake, which occurred in Uzziah's reign; cf. the later echo of this event in Zechariah 14:5). I regard this book as representing an effort to put the whole realm of prophecy on a serious historical basis. Many of the oracular utterances of the prophets had to do with predictions and fulfillments (whether conditional or not), and much of the tradition was anecdotal and legendary (cf. the stories about the earlier prophets, especially Elijah and Elisha). The arena was overcrowded with all kinds of prophets, most of them phonies. Thus, through the publication of a book with explicit warnings and predictions, tied to real events, the words of a prophet could be tested against the historical events that followed. The fact that there is relatively low-level correlation between prophecy and prediction (with considerable divergence in detail, although obviously there is correspondence in broad categories or the books would not be in the Bible at all) shows that the scribes and editors were faithful in their task and didn't tamper much with the material. If they had, then the prophets would come off a lot better in averages and details. Thus, for the most part, Amos's great oracles against the nations were not fulfilled, at least not within a credible range of time (i.e., a generation at most). While the fall of Israel ultimately vindicated his judgments, the survival of several of the other nations for a much longer period did not, and especially the rescue of Judah and Jerusalem. So we may be sure that Amos actually said most of those things, and also that the scribes were faithful in preserving what he said, regardless of what actually happened later. From this beginning we see the rise of other prophets of the same century with similar messages about the Northern and Southern Kingdoms.

Micah's famous prophecy about the destruction of Jerusalem is a remarkable case in point: he must have said just those words in 3:12 (quoted almost verbatim by Jeremiah in chap. 26 a century or so later), and they were just as certainly not fulfilled, certainly not within any normal expectation. Far from discrediting the prophet, however, Jeremiah explains that everyone understood that because Hezekiah and the people repented, Jerusalem was spared and the prophecy remained unfulfilled. The outcome is not in the hands or words of the prophet, but with God, and the prediction is always subject to reversal or modification depending on what transpires between humans and the deity. The eighth-century collection is just such a thanksgiving directed at the deity who spared Jerusalem through the repentance of Hezekiah and the intercession of Isaiah, a climactic point in the history of the nation and of prophecy (2 Kings 18–19; cf. Isaiah 36–37). The collection is full of warnings based on the experience of Israel (the Northern Kingdom), which was warned and threatened, and did not repent and was destroyed (cf. Amos, Hosea, Isaiah, Micah, and also 2 Kings 17, which explains the whole experience). Jerusalem, on the other hand, was similarly warned and threatened, but did repent, and therefore was spared. Clearly the motivation is Judahite, and the intention is to glorify not only God, but also the dynast who was faithful in his duty and was therefore rewarded by keeping his kingdom—while the Assyrians went home without destroying the city or terminating the dynasty, which would have been their normal practice in dealing with rebellious vassals.

We can also speak of a seventh to sixth century assemblage, which was based on the earlier collection and which reflected the reversal of Jerusalem's destiny. Just as Samaria had been destroyed earlier, so now that fate would overtake the sister city, in spite of the warnings and threats uttered by prophets such as Jeremiah, Ezekiel, and others from that period. In short, this was Act II in the drama: the first act marked the end of the Northern Kingdom and the sparing of the Southern Kingdom; the second act saw the end of the Southern Kingdom. Here we rely on books such as Jeremiah and Ezekiel, which are clearly exilic in date in their final form. Although these books reflect the history of Israel and Judah up to that point, they also make a place for a future and inject an element of hope and confidence in a restoration that is largely lacking from the Primary History, although present in the Chronicler's Work.[14] These books, including Jeremiah, Ezekiel, and the others that could be associated with them, belong to the second tier, and doubtless were joined to the first group to produce a sixth-century collection of Major and Minor Prophets. Dates have been suggested for the books of Jeremiah and Ezekiel, and the others probably belong to the same period.

Finally, we have a post-exilic group, including Second Isaiah and the last three books in the collection of the Twelve. Here the major new emphasis is on the return, reported in glowing terms by Second Isaiah and, more prosaically perhaps, by Zechariah and

Haggai. In any case, a dramatic turn of events had to be reflected in the prophetic utterances, and the unknown prophet of the exile is clearly the chief spokesman of this group. While there is a good deal of prose in Haggai and Zechariah (as also in Ezekiel and Jeremiah), Second Isaiah is a throwback to the earlier period of poetic prophetic oracles. In any case, this group represents the third phase of the Latter Prophets, and with the reestablishment of the exiles in their land and the rebuilding of the Temple and the City, the story effectively comes to an end. This is also true of the Hebrew Bible as a whole. With the era of Ezra and Nehemiah the curtain comes down on prophecy and on the history of the Jews. The Book of Daniel is a dramatic exception and deserves independent treatment, both because it comes from a later period and reflects the Greek era, and because it shows a fourth phase of prophecy (apocalyptic)—which is no longer classical prophecy at all, although disguised as such.

The four books (or scrolls) of the Latter Prophets match up well against the four books of the Former Prophets in overall length (the totals are about 70,000 words each, with the Latter Prophets running a little higher than the Former Prophets):

Former Prophets		Latter Prophets	
Joshua	10,051	Isaiah	16,933
Judges	9,885	Jeremiah	21,835
Samuel	24,301	Ezekiel	18,730
Kings	25,421	Minor Prophets	14,355
	69,658		71,853

The juxtaposition and organization of the materials reflect an interest in overall balance and symmetry, but the individual books vary widely in length, showing that other factors were operative in determining their scope and length. As it happens, both the two shortest and two longest of the books (ranging from 10,000 to 25,000 words) are in the Former Prophets, while the books of the Latter Prophets are closer in length, from Jeremiah with nearly 22,000 words to the Minor Prophets with over 14,000. We have adopted or accepted the traditional or standard order of these books for our purposes, which puts Isaiah first, followed by Jeremiah, Ezekiel, and the Book of the Twelve—an arrangement reflecting the presumed chronological order of the major prophets. A case can also be made, however, for another order, beginning with Jeremiah, followed by Ezekiel and Isaiah, and ending, as always, with the Book of the Twelve.[15] The rationale for this sequence is not chronology but size, the largest or longest book coming first, and the rest following according to size. This type of arrangement is also present in the ordering of the smaller units or chapters (suras) of the Qu'ran, the holy book of Islam. Thus, although Isaiah has sixty-six chapters, and Jeremiah and Ezekiel fifty-two and forty-eight, respectively, chapters are not a reliable criterion for measuring quantity, since they vary so much in length. Now that we have accurate word counts for all of the books of the Hebrew Bible (see Lecture 1, note 2), we are in a much better position to compare them with each other. It may be added that the book of the Latter Prophets with the most chapters has the fewest number of words: the Minor Prophets with 67 chapters and only 14,355 words. Such an arrangement would emphasize the importance and centrality of the two major prophets of the Fall of Jerusalem and the Babylonian Exile—Jeremiah and Ezekiel—and then proceed to fill in the fuller picture of anterior and posterior events provided by the remaining prophetic books.

The standard order would build up the story from the antecedents in the eighth century with the prophetic activity of Isaiah, before proceeding with the two great central prophets, Jeremiah and Ezekiel. Once again, the Book of the Twelve serves to fill in the centuries and fill out the picture with the oracles and stories of numerous other prophets.

No simple system or analysis works well, since the books themselves are heterogeneous and there are inevitable anomalies and discrepancies. Thus, in the traditional order, while Isaiah precedes Jeremiah and Ezekiel, we also have Second Isaiah (Isaiah 34–35, 40–66), which refers to and depicts events and situations later than and beyond the reach of Jeremiah and Ezekiel. At the same time, the Book of the Twelve stands apart from the other books because it begins (chronologically) before Isaiah and ends later than the other books. In this case, chronology was overridden by convenience, or rather by the necessity of lumping together or assembling in a single book all the minor prophetic works, the majority of which are less than 1,000 words and the longest of which barely exceeds 3,000 words (Zechariah at 3,128). While short books could be written on separate scrolls, as we know from the example of the *megillot* in the third part of the Canon, such a procedure would not have served the purposes of the compiler, who was working with a symmetrical plan consisting of eight books, evenly divided (four and four) and of matching length.

Our proposal for ordering or interpreting the existing arrangement of the books is more complex since we attempt to incorporate and account for the variety of data in the separate books and how they relate to form a coherent whole. To begin with, we follow the traditional order in recognizing that the Major Prophets are placed chronologically: Isaiah in the eighth century, Jeremiah in the seventh to sixth, and Ezekiel slightly later. In corresponding manner, the Minor Prophets are arranged chronologically as well, although the compiler may have had difficulty in deciding or defending a decision in a number of cases. In general, however, the earliest works, such as Amos, Hosea, and Micah, come at the front end, while the later post-exilic books are at the end of the sequence.

Our model, which may be described as a series of concentric circles with some interlocking rings and spiral binders, depends for its definition on the dates (exact and approximate) in the books themselves to determine the order and relationships. Thus Ezekiel extends over the shortest time span, from the fifth to the twenty-seventh (or possibly thirtieth) year of the exile (or ca. 593/2–571/0 [or 568/7] B.C.E.), barely covering the active ministry of the prophet.[16] Surrounding this concentrated core—which includes and pinpoints the central event of the prophetic corpus, the capture of Jerusalem and the destruction of the Temple—is the Book of Jeremiah, whose dates include the period covered by Ezekiel and extend some years beyond in both directions. Thus Jeremiah begins with the call of the prophet (1:2) in the thirteenth year of Josiah's reign (628/7 B.C.E.), and it ends with the historical summary in chapter 52 (repeated in 2 Kings 25), the final date being the thirty-seventh year of the exile, or 561/0 B.C.E. The horizon or field of vision has been extended from a maximum of twenty-five years to about sixty-seven years—the latter forming an envelope around the former, thereby increasing the emphasis and sharpening the focus on the central event.

Turning then to the Book of Isaiah, we find in the vision of chapter 6 the earliest attested date—the year that King Uzziah died, or ca. 740 B.C.E. There is no corresponding concluding date at the end of the book, but some clues are offered in later chapters. Chapter 39 offers data concerning the closing years of Hezekiah's reign (down to 697/6 or 687/6, depending on whose chronology we follow)[17] that would suffice for the ministry or prophetic career of Isaiah only; it does not take into account the activities of the more mysterious figure of Second Isaiah (or additional prophet) whose work is now subjoined to that of the First Isaiah. Since, however, we are dealing in the first (and last) instance with books and not just persons, we must extend the scope of the time frame to include the beginning of the Persian era. While no exact dates are given, the clearest clue we have is the mention of Cyrus in chapters 44–45, and we can therefore suggest a date around 540 B.C.E. for the latter part (chaps. 40–66) of Isaiah. Most scholars would extend the chronology further to accommodate a commonly postulated Third Isaiah, which may reflect some experience in the Holy Land after the return from exile.[18] However, I prefer to keep to the more conservative dating. In any case, it is clear that the Book of Isaiah forms a third circle, or envelope, around the other two books and extends the scope of the combined works by an additional one hundred years at the front end, and by at least twenty years or so at the lower end of the scale, ca. 740–540 B.C.E.

We can also offer a partial explanation for the curious composite character of this book. Most scholarly attention over the years has been devoted to the question of and debate over the unity of authorship, and whether the eighth-century prophet of Jerusalem could somehow have propelled himself into the sixth century in order to compose orally or in written form the oracles (34–35, 40–66), which clearly deal with the end of the Babylonian Captivity and the return of the Holy Land under the sponsorship of the Persian emperor, Cyrus the Great. Consequently, less attention has been given to the question of literary connection or unity of these segments. On the one hand, First Isaiah deals with the events of the period from about 740 to 701 and beyond, events occurring during the lifetime of the prophet.[19] This unit (chaps. 1–33, 36–39) concludes with a prose narrative (chaps. 36–39), partly derived from a similar section in 2 Kings (chaps. 18–20); this section shows that a prior edition of Isaiah was issued—perhaps in the seventh century or perhaps when the D-Work was completed in the sixth century. In this edition, Isaiah's role in the deliverance of Jerusalem was duly noted and the important prediction recorded that Hezekiah's descendants would serve the King of Babylon—a prophecy fulfilled in the days of Nebuchadnezzar when Jehoiachin and Zedekiah were vassal-kings, and when Jehoiachin was a prisoner in Babylon.

Second Isaiah picks up the story toward the end of the exile and speaks of the imminent return, perhaps also reflecting the early stages of that return under Cyrus, who is mentioned by name. Thus in its present form, the Book of Isaiah provides a frame around the central and crucial event of the Fall of Jerusalem, but curiously refers to that event either as a future possibility (First Isaiah) or as an event of the past (Second Isaiah). There is no description of the event itself, which would be very strange if the book were considered by itself. In the larger configuration, however, it is bound to the other major prophets in the Prophetic Corpus, not to mention the Twelve Minor Prophets. Jeremiah and Ezekiel, especially, supply the missing datum in great detail and fill in the material missing from the Book of Isaiah. Thus, if we read the books in the following order—First Isaiah (1–33, 36–39), Jeremiah, Ezekiel, Second Isaiah (34–35, 40–66)—we would have the story in the right order and all the parts would fit. Since the compiler was acting under various constraints, some of which are not readily discernible, the actual order is different from what we have suggested. In any case, however, it is striking that Jeremiah and Ezekiel supply precisely the information lacking in Isaiah, whereas Isaiah provides the framework within which the books of Jeremiah and Ezekiel can best be understood. The Book of the Twelve likewise fills in other gaps and is itself supplemented by the Major Prophets. Taking them all together, we can work out a fairly complete and much fuller account of the eighth to sixth centuries than we have in the D- or C-Works, although the latter, in turn, provide the structure into which the Latter Prophets fit and to which they belong.

When it comes to the Book of the Twelve, we find the same phenomenon. Since twelve separate works are involved, the spread can be and is the greatest of all the books; this last segment of the series forms the largest and most comprehensive frame, beginning earlier than the others and ending later, while filling in gaps or reinforcing coverage at several points along the way. While precise dates for the earliest prophets are unavailable, we can place Amos and Hosea in the overlapping reigns of Jeroboam II in the North and Uzziah in the South, roughly the first half of the eighth century B.C.E. In my opinion, the prophetic activity of Amos belongs earlier rather than later in the reigns of those two kings;[20] I would tentatively assign a date in the first quarter of the eighth century B.C.E. to the beginning of the Book of the Twelve, and hence for the Latter Prophets as a whole. At the other extreme, in Zechariah 7:1 we have a final fixed date for the Book of the Twelve: the fourth year of Darius I (518/17 B.C.E.). It is reasonable to extend the period further, especially regarding the Book of Malachi, which is generally dated in the fifth century, around the time of Ezra-Nehemiah, or even later. For our purposes it is sufficient to establish a closing date in the final quarter of the sixth century. Thus the Minor Prophets and the Latter Prophets, as a whole, encompass a critical period in Israel's history, like an inset in a larger map, with increasingly detailed and specific presentation of the central data, climaxing and culminating in the death of the nation and destruction of its capital city. In this way the Latter

Prophets are tied most closely with the Primary History, which also has its culmination in the fall of the city and the end of the nation.

At the same time, the Latter Prophets put the whole affair in another and quite different light, and with respect to the return and restoration, they have affinities with and ties to the third part of the Hebrew Bible—the Writings—and, in particular, the Chronicler's Work. As already noted, the Latter Prophets form a bridge between the Primary History and the Writings, but especially to the C-Work with which, in the best codices, the Writings or Ketubim begin and end.

The Latter Prophets cover a period of at least 250 years, from the first part of the eighth century to the last part of the sixth century, and possibly a longer period (up to 300 years or more, depending on how far into the fifth century one is prepared to go to include the latter part of Zechariah [9–14] and Malachi); there are also editorial insertions and additions at other places. Some scholars have suggested and argued that certain materials (e.g., in Hosea) belong to an earlier period, and thus that the coverage should be extended backward as well as forward in time. For the great bulk of the material, however, the dates provided by the literature itself will suffice.

As already noted, the purpose of this collection was not only to supplement and expand the treatment of the central issue—the destruction of nation, city, and temple—but also to provide a different perspective, one that shows not only the sequence of events and oracles leading up to the catastrophe, but also what happened afterward: the exile, the return and the restoration, the renewal of life in the city, and the rebuilding and dedication of the Second Temple. So it is much more than simply an expansion or elaboration of the Primary History. Not only does it carry the story down to a new point—one that is very different from the end of the Primary History, where everything is in ruins and the people are dispersed among the nations—but it puts the events more sharply and clearly in the context and framework of prophetic utterance and interpretation. All history, and especially that of Israel, is presented theologically in the Bible, but there is a difference between the presentation by the historians of the Primary History and that of the compilers of the Latter Prophets. In the former we have in good part a retrospective survey of the decisive events in Israel's past, interpreted in the light of central themes in its religion. In the latter, we are closer to the action; in many cases the words of the prophets show them actively participating in the events themselves and providing the direct channel of communication between God and his people. We must not exaggerate the differences, since there was agreement on the essentials of the faith based on the old traditions, and mutual influence in both directions. Nevertheless, the prophets stand out, not only as exceptional individuals in the history of Israel, but especially as the direct link between God and his people and as mediators of the survival and revival of Israel. They were credited, not just with having perceived and announced the forthcoming destruction of the nation, but with having explained suitably and acceptably the reasons and process, thereby confirming their credentials and status. More important was their role in preserving a nucleus and preparing survivors for return, restoration, and renewal—all duly promised by the same deity who had wreaked devastation on them. When compared with other peoples that suffered the same or a similar fate, the difference for Israel was its prophets, and it was they who ensured a return and renewal. So far as we know, no other nation had the same experience and no other nation had prophets like those of Israel. The correlation seems both reasonable and inevitable, and it is precisely in the books of the Latter Prophets that the vital difference is to be found.

Taking the Latter Prophets as a group—organized and arranged by an editor or editors in the form in which they have come down to us, in their final canonical structure—we can discuss the major themes and elements, the flow or movement from beginning to end, and identify the purpose and objectives of the whole. By including both anterior and posterior events, the editor(s) could put the central event (the destruction of Jerusalem) into perspective, tracing the historical origins of the threat to Jerusalem's existence back to the Assyrian campaigns of the latter half of the eighth century. At the same time, they could also show that, in spite of the structure of the Primary History, the story did not end with defeat and destruction; rather, after a pause, namely the Babylonian Captivity, a new era would and did begin with return, restoration, and rebuilding. While the latter process had not come full circle with the restoration of an independent kingdom and a royal ruler of the House of David on the throne, the basic moves had been made, and the achievements by the end of the era of the Latter Prophets were not inconsiderable. After all, we could hardly expect that conditions and circumstances at the end would be the same as at the beginning. The prophets, their secretaries, and the editors were dealing with historical realities, not making up fairy tales. The outlook was essentially favorable; those responsible for this great work could be satisfied that in the essentials and according to their principles, the prophets had done their work and helped to create a unique reality in the ancient Near East, a community almost literally brought back from the dead, to appeal once more to Ezekiel's vivid and memorable parable.

We can thus divide and arrange the prophetic books into three groups according to a time-line:

1. The antecedent events: the eighth century. We can classify four prophets under this heading:

    Kings

Judah	*Israel*
Uzziah	Jeroboam
Jotham	
Ahaz	
Hezekiah	

    Prophets

Major	*Minor*
1 Isaiah	Amos
	Hosea
	Micah

2. The central events leading to the fall of Jerusalem and the Babylonian Exile: late seventh to early sixth century.

Kings
Judah
Josiah
Jehoahaz
Jehoiakim
Jehoiakin and Zedekiah

Prophets

Major	*Minor*
Jeremiah	Nahum
Ezekiel	Zephaniah
	Habakkuk
	Obadiah

Perhaps we should include here Joel and Jonah as well, although their dates remain uncertain.

3. The third phase concerns the return from exile and the rebuilding of the city and temple. The dates here are from the last years of the exile, perhaps beginning around 550 and continuing at least to 518/7, or perhaps further toward the end of the sixth century or into the fifth century B.C.E.

Prophets

Major	*Minor*
2 Isaiah	Haggai
3 Isaiah (?)	Zechariah
	Malachi

I. The Eighth Century

It has been a commonplace of biblical scholarship of the past century that the prophets of the eighth century marked a turning point in Israelite religion and introduced new ideas, doctrines, and conceptions. They have been hailed as creators, or at least definers, of ethical monotheism with extensive implications for the development of biblical thought and the religions that stem from the Bible. There can be little doubt that these and the other great prophets of Israel and Judah left a permanent stamp on the religion that they inherited and the community in which they lived. It is very much in our interest to determine just what they intended and accomplished, without exaggerating the timelessness and universality of their message, or minimizing the local and time-conditioned aspects of their work. Their intention, clearly, was not to utter timeless truths about God, the universe, and the world, but rather to deliver the divine message to people in a specific historical nexus—not that the two objectives are entirely incompatible or that the second could not also embrace the first. What we wish to show is how the message of the prophets met the situation and what came out of the interaction.

Beginning with Amos and Hosea, we (and Israel) hear, for the first time, a direct threat to the existence of the nation(s). It is stated unambiguously in the opening speech by Amos, and similarly in Hosea. Thus, the stage is set for the onslaught that will overwhelm first the Northern Kingdom and ultimately the Southern Kingdom as well. The threat is framed in terms of divine judgment, but political-military factors and details are supplied as well. The God of the whole earth, and in particular of the land between the great empires—Assyria to the northeast and Egypt to the southwest, now occupied by not fewer than eight small nations—has passed judgment on all eight nations: these nations will be overrun and all of the incumbent powers and countries will be wiped out—an old era ended and a new age begun. All of this was fresh and new and previously unheard from prophetic lips.[21]

Earlier prophets, such as Samuel and Ahijah, or even Elijah and Elisha of the preceding century, had been wrapped up in local and national affairs, concerned about the faith and fealty of rulers and subjects, but not with the grand international designs of the deity. While the threat posed by neighboring peoples, such as the Philistines or Aramaeans, was not trivial, it also was not regarded as lethal. When a major power, such as Assyria, loomed on the horizon, and when its objectives became clear, then all the small nations between Assyria and its ultimate target, Egypt, were at risk and in grave jeopardy. It is an unmentioned tribute to their skill in international politics and military tactics, and to the prowess of both Israel and Judah and their leaders, that the two nations held out as long as they did in the face of such overwhelming power. For the prophets and the biblical writers generally, however, that was emphatically not the prime or central issue. They viewed the situation through theological eyes and saw the issues in terms of national morality, i.e., the fidelity of the community to the terms of the covenant, and in terms of loyalty and obedience to their God. The challenge would be joined and resolved not on the battlefield or in the "conference room," but in the behavior and intentions of the people. For Amos, Hosea, and the others, that issue had been settled; judgment could and must be pronounced. For three gross violations, yea for four, Israel and Judah would be punished (Amos 2:4–16). The rest of the story—the oracles and pronouncements of the prophets—leads to the edge of doom. By the end of the eighth century, Israel and its capital city, Samaria, had fallen to the Assyrians, and the kingdom had been permanently destroyed, carved up into imperial provinces. Judah had also been overrun and Jerusalem put under siege by the armies of Sennacherib. At the last moment, deliverance came, and the city and nation were spared—although Hezekiah was forced to pay a huge indemnity and submit to the authority of the Assyrian overlord.[22]

For prophets and kings, historians and theologians, the lesson of the eighth century was clear and unmistakable: Israel and Judah were guilty of high crimes against the covenant with God, and both were under judgment of death for these violations—a judgment to be carried out by the Assyrian horde, "the rod of my anger." Israel persisted in its sinful and criminal activity, stubbornly resisted the warnings and pleadings of the prophets sent to it, and suffered the consequences: the destruction and irreversible dissolution of the nation. In the words of the prophet Amos, "the virgin Israel had fallen, not to rise again" (Amos 5:2). Judah, on the other hand, under the same sentence of death, repented under the leadership of the pious king Hezekiah and, through the mediation of the faithful prophet Isaiah, was spared by divine intervention. As a result, the Assyrians withdrew, the city and state survived, and the king remained on his throne.

For the later prophets, the experience of the eighth century was both a model and lesson. In the face of deserved judgment there is only one recourse: total truthful repentance. The separate fates of the two nations prove the point. If you repent, then God will repent and withhold the punishment. But the threat remains and the second act in the drama bears out that fact.

II. The Seventh to Sixth Centuries

A century later, Judah was again threatened with disaster, this time at the hands of the Babylonians, who had supplanted the Assyrians as the dominant power in the Near East. After an initial phase of submission, Jehoiakim, the king, and the leadership of Judah rebelled against Nebuchadnezzar and promptly paid the penalty: loss of independence and surrender of the city to the Babylonian king. The king of Judah died, and his son Jehoiachin inherited the throne only long enough to surrender and go into captivity. An uncle, Zedekiah, the last surviving son of Josiah, was put on the throne as a vassal and puppet, and Judah was given a last chance for survival. Jeremiah preached regularly and repeatedly that submission to Babylon was the only viable policy, along with repentance and rigorous adherence to the covenant. Otherwise, disaster loomed. In a similar situation, the only course of action was to emulate Hezekiah and the people of an earlier time in the hope that Judah would again be spared. Ezekiel's views were much the same, although he believed that the time for remedial action was rapidly disappearing, if it was not already too late for those in Jerusalem and Judah. In fact, it was. Zedekiah revolted in a last desperate effort to regain independence for Judah, as his father, the eminent Josiah had done. Like Josiah, however, he was defeated, and ultimately died in exile. The nation was no more; this time the city and temple were destroyed, and the remainder of the leadership was also taken away. The fate of Samaria had been visited upon Jerusalem, and once again the prophets were vindicated as bearers of the divine message of warning, threat, and judgment.[23]

III. The Sixth to Fifth Centuries

Phase three overlaps with phase two; once the exile began and the end had come to the nation, there were stirrings of hope for the future. The same prophets who had warned of destruction and lived to see their predictions come true now promised survival of the exiles and restoration to and of the homeland. While such reassurances and forecasts may be secondary accretions in some of the earlier prophets (i.e., those of the eighth century) in order to have as many prophets as possible fit a common pattern, it is difficult to accept the view of some scholars that all such adumbrations of a brighter future are the work of exilic and post-exilic editors. Certainly with Jeremiah and Ezekiel, we have every reason to believe that, while the cause of those who remained behind with Zedekiah proved hopeless, there was ample justification to encourage those in exile to hold fast to the faith and to pray for a better future. The fact that neither of the predictions (the length of the exile or the period of Babylonian oppression) came true in any precise way, or was on target with respect to the way in which the redemption and release were carried out, is negative evidence for their authenticity. No one, in antiquity at least, invented false prophecies after the facts were known.

If prophets such as Jeremiah and Ezekiel paved the way for the return and provided the encouragement and counsel for those in exile, we must look to other prophets who ushered in the new era. The role of men such as Haggai and Zechariah is amply attested; their oracles concerning the returned exiles and the rebuilding of the Temple are recorded in the books that bear their names. Pride of place belongs to Second Isaiah, however, as the moving spirit behind the return. It is he who identifies Cyrus the Great as the anointed of the Lord who is to carry out this task as part of a worldwide plan of the deity, and so fulfill the divine intention regarding his own special people. The return under the Edict of Cyrus is amply documented in the C-Work, as are the roles of Haggai and Zechariah in exhorting the people to complete the task begun some years earlier. Thus we can trace parallel developments between Second Isaiah and Haggai-Zechariah on the one hand, and Chronicles and Ezra-Nehemiah on the other—just as was the case with the Primary History and the prophecies of Isaiah and Jeremiah, among others. It would be plausible to associate the oracles of Malachi with the period of Ezra and Nehemiah, although it is difficult to show any direct connections or correlations. While they deal with similar subjects, there is no mention of authentic prophets in the days of either of these Persian-sponsored administrators. So it is more likely that Malachi comes from a somewhat earlier period.[24]

From first to last, the Latter Prophets present a dual theme that spells out the relationship between Israel and its God, and the historical consequences of attitudes and behavior on both sides. Amos expresses the essential paradox in classical and unforgettable words:

You only have I known among all the clans of the earth.
Therefore, I will punish you for all your iniquities. (3:2)

The special status of Israel in relation to its God ensures that it will be judged and punished for its sins and covenant violations. The relationship is morally conditioned. Otherwise, it would only be one more of the special relationships between all the nations and their gods—relationships in which a universal morality or ethic plays no role at all. At the same time, the relationship is special, if not unique, and the same God who necessarily judges and punishes, must and will renew and restore. The moral tone and component are not vitiated, but the prior, basic, underlying, and overriding commitment of deity to people persists and will overcome all obstacles. Ezekiel (36–37) expresses the paradox in the most dramatic language that is presented throughout the corpus: the same God who imposed the death sentence and executed capital punishment on his own people will nevertheless bring them back to life, restore them to their land and their land to them, and also ensure that such a calamity will never happen again by instilling a new spirit in them so that he or they can and will live together in harmony and peace on the land that is sacred to both parties. Jeremiah (31:31–40) says the same thing in different words when describing the new covenant that will bind God to his people and his people to him forever, and without the possibility of the kind of breach that brought disaster on them in the recent past.

Now there are a couple of other points to be made about connections between the Latter Prophets and other parts of the Hebrew Bible. As already noted in the first lecture, the Primary History consists of two well-defined units, each with a distinctive style and vocabulary, while nevertheless comprising an overall unity and narrative continuity. The first four books make up the P-Work (Priestly Work) and the last five make up the D-Work (Deuteronomic Work). That is the simplest form of the analysis, although some scholars believe they can detect traces or elements of the D-Work in earlier books, while an older and still viable analysis assigns at least parts of Joshua to the P-Work.[25]

Regardless of these nuances or details, the sharply delineated differences between these two massive works ensure the reliability of the foregoing analysis. Few, if any, scholars have any difficulty in differentiating P from D. Equally impressive and widely acknowledged is the correlation between each of these works and that of a major prophet. The affinities between the D-Work and the Book of Jeremiah on the one hand, and between the P-Work and Ezekiel on the other, are notable and important. While I think it would be going too far to attribute the D-Work to Jeremiah (see note 5 of this lecture for reference), there is no doubt that an important link exists between them, and a deliberate connection has been made by attaching a version of the last chapter of 2 Kings to the end of Jeremiah (chap. 52). In this case we have a likely culprit or candidate: the scribe Baruch. He is credited with copying down some of Jeremiah's oracles to which "many words like them were also added" (Jeremiah 36:32). It would be entirely reasonable for Baruch, who edited and produced at least some version of the Book of Jeremiah, to also have had an important hand in the production of the D-Work. The point of the argument is that the closest affinities are to be found between the prose passages in Jeremiah and the D-Work, which is almost entirely in prose. We may suppose that Baruch copied down the poetic oracles of the prophet through oral dictation, but that he himself was responsible for the prose narratives concerning Jeremiah and other passages of similar nature in the book.

It would appear then that the Deuteronomic group co-opted the prophet or claimed him as a leader, a modern representative of the prophetic movement whose archetype was Moses himself, the unique prophet of Israel. The association would be a natural one, and there is no reason to doubt that Jeremiah would have lent his name and prestige to such a group, to which he himself may well have belonged by professional and family ties. The movement was led by priests, but more likely the rural or non-temple priests, a group to which Jeremiah belonged.[26]

The same sort of hypothesis can be proposed for the link between Ezekiel and the P-Work. Certainly the prophet was not the editor of the P-Work, since his own book differs sharply with the latter on many important points of worship and law. These differences caused the rabbis considerable difficulty in later times as they attempted to reconcile divergent and discordant regulations and prescriptions.[27] Nevertheless, there are important links between the works, especially in style and vocabulary as well as general outlook and perhaps dates. So we may suppose that the Priestly Group that promulgated the P-Work, and perhaps the Primary History as a whole, co-opted Ezekiel and his work for their objectives. Again we note that Ezekiel, too, was a priest (Ezekiel 1:3), and that he probably belonged to the Temple priesthood in contrast with Jeremiah. It may finally be nothing more than coincidence, but it would appear that strong forces were at work in linking Jeremiah and the D-Work, and Ezekiel and the P-Work, in the compilation and canonization of the combined P and D works in the Primary History and in the inclusion of both Jeremiah and Ezekiel in the Latter Prophets of the same canon. It should be remembered that the work of a prophet is likely to be individualistic and idiosyncratic, whereas an official history or book of rules is likely to be the work of a scribe or scribes representing a consensus.

There remains the Book of Isaiah, and for it we propose a link with the remaining prose history, the C-Work. Here the connection is not so much a matter of style or of contemporary date, since both works are somewhat heterogeneous and composite, but rather of theme and outlook. Since the Book of Isaiah consists of at least two main parts, we should look for two principal points of contact.

As Halpern has pointed out (see note 9 of this lecture), one of the chief heroes of the C-Work is King Hezekiah of Judah, and it is possible that an early version of the C-Work culminated with the reign of that king. According to the traditions in Isaiah, Kings, and Chronicles, there was a close association between king and prophet that resulted in the miraculous deliverance of the city and the kingdom from the siege imposed by Sennacherib in 701. From this we conclude that Isaiah was the prophet of choice of the C-Work, and he may even have had a connection with those courtiers responsible for an early version of it. This early version was basically a dynastic history of the House of David, to which the prophet also was partial, although in a rather ambivalent way, but that seems to have been true of prophets generally. Other major emphases in the C-Work concern the city of Jerusalem and the Temple, matters in which Isaiah also shows considerable interest.

At the other end of the Book of Isaiah, we find oracles dealing with the return from exile. In particular, hopes are expressed about the role of Cyrus in sponsoring this return and in the rebuilding of the Temple (Isaiah 45). As we have seen, these same elements turn up in the C-Work, especially at the end of 2 Chronicles and the beginning of the Book of Ezra. The links are impressive, since nowhere else in the Hebrew Bible is Cyrus mentioned in connection with the return from exile and the rebuilding of the Temple.

In the final edition of the C-Work the connection with Second Isaiah is made, just as the link with First Isaiah was developed in an earlier version.

Our proposal is that there are demonstrable links between the books of the major prophets and the historical works known to us in the Bible. We can connect Jeremiah and Ezekiel with various parts of the Primary History, while there are links between Isaiah (First and Second) and the Chronicler's Work. All this points to the intricate and interlocking character of the Hebrew Bible and supports the view that a single mind or compatible group was at work in collecting, compiling, organizing, and arranging the component parts into a coherent whole.

The Writings

The Writings (Hebrew *kĕtûbîm*) constitute the third main part of the Hebrew Bible, and as the name indicates, this group of books is the most diverse and heterogeneous of all. Nevertheless, we believe that an overall compiler or editor has been at work here as well, and without tampering with the contents or integrity of the separate works, has achieved a certain cohesion and unity through careful selection and arrangement of the parts. While the order of the books varies somewhat in the different manuscripts and traditions, we may begin our survey with the order preserved in the standard printed Hebrew Bibles. In this arrangement of the Hebrew Bible, the Ketubim begin with the three poetic works: Psalms, Job, and Proverbs (the order of the three books varies in different manuscripts). It then continues with the Five Rolls or *mĕgillôt* (short books written on separate scrolls): Ruth, Song of Songs (Canticles), Ecclesiastes (Koheleth), Lamentations, and Esther. The order is roughly chronological (in terms of contents), and the five together could easily be accommodated in a single scroll of moderate size (about 10,000 words in all). These are followed in turn by the Book of Daniel and the Chronicler's Work. The last consists of 1 and 2 Chronicles (originally a single book and written on a single scroll) and Ezra-Nehemiah (also originally a single book).[1] They are placed in reverse order, however, or not in the normal or expected chronological sequence; the narrative would require Chronicles to be followed by Ezra-Nehemiah. The reverse order places Ezra-Nehemiah first, followed by Chronicles, thus producing an odd circular effect if the books are read consecutively. In this present order, the Chronicler's Work begins with the account of the Edict of Cyrus, in which the Jews in captivity were not only permitted but encouraged to return to their homeland in Judah and also to rebuild the Temple in Jerusalem. The narrative continues to the end of Ezra-Nehemiah; then it begins all over again at the beginning of Chronicles with Adam and the genealogies derived from the Book of Genesis. The whole history of the people is covered once more, with particular emphasis on Judah from the time of the accession of David until the end of the kingdom. Then the last entry in Chronicles repeats the Edict of Cyrus to the Jews in captivity with which Ezra-Nehemiah began, thus forming an envelope around the whole work and echoing an event of central importance to the author or editor.

This inverted arrangement is curious, to say the least, and it is not surprising to find other arrangements of these books.[2] In the Greek tradition, the Chronicler's Work is placed after the Books of 1 and 2 Kings (actually Kingdoms or Reigns) and the sequence is normal. We may suppose that the original form of the Chronicler's Work was in consecutive order, but then one might wonder about the repetition of the paragraph with which Chronicles ends and Ezra-Nehemiah begins. The books of the Primary History follow in sequence without such obvious linkage. It would seem that the repetition of this paragraph in the Hebrew Bible, while perhaps a secondary development, points to a physical separation of the two books so as to remind the reader of their connection and at the same time emphasize a point of interest and importance to the compiler/editor.

While the arrangement in the standard editions exhibits a structural curiosity or literary device of some interest, the arrangement in the oldest and best of the extant medieval codices, Aleppo and Leningrad, offers a rationale for the separation of the two parts and their connection as well. Instead of being at the end of the Writings, Chronicles is at the beginning of this whole unit, thus making Ezra-Nehemiah the last book of the section and of the Bible itself. The Chronicler's Work, therefore, forms an envelope around the Writings, encompassing all of the other books previously mentioned and constituting a unifying and ordering framework for them. At the same time, the connection between the two works is stressed by the repetition of the paragraph that comes at the end of Chronicles and that is unique to this work, since it does not occur in the Books of 1 and 2 Kings. At the beginning of Ezra-Nehemiah, we find the same paragraph as an echo, reminding the reader that Ezra-Nehemiah is the sequel to or continuation of the book with which the section opened. The idea inherent in the arrangement—namely, that the Chronicler's Work encompasses the interior works—is also appropriate with respect to their contents and themes. Thus, the Chronicler's Work covers the whole span of the Hebrew Bible, from the beginning to the present day (the time of Ezra-Nehemiah), and everything within the framework fits into that time span. More than this, the major themes and emphases in the Chronicler's Work are exemplified in the other associated works.

The main figures in the Chronicler's Work are David and Solomon on one side, and Moses (and Aaron and the priesthood) on the other. Traditionally, the Book of Job was attributed to Moses, along with the Pentateuch, so its inclusion in the Canon was assured by the association with that venerable figure. Other books, such as Psalms and Proverbs, apart from being reflections of sacred practice and institutions in Temple and Palace, were ascribed to dominant figures in the story—David and Solomon, i.e., the Psalms of David and the Proverbs of Solomon.[3] These latter associations do not end with those books but continue with the *megillot*, or Rolls. The first three—Ruth, Song of Songs, and Ecclesiastes—are all directly and deliberately connected with the House of David. The first is somewhat unusual, since it purports to describe the history of David's ancestors (Ruth was his great-grandmother and could have lived to see him born), while both of the others are attributed to Solomon. We have, therefore, in the Writings a heavy concentration of works connected with or attributed to the House of David.

The remaining rolls include Lamentations, which echoes another important theme of the Chronicler's Work and the Primary History: the destruction of the City of Jerusalem and its Temple, and the terrible tragedy of 587/6 B.C.E. It provides a salutary reminder of the dark downside of that central and decisive experience. While the Chronicler's Work, in contrast with the Primary History, emphasizes the continuity of the people and the persistence of the divine commitment to land, city, and temple, the devastation and destruction serve to highlight the constancy of God and his persistence in restoring and maintaining his people. Finally, the Book of Esther fills in the gap between the first generation of those who returned from exile under the leadership of Zerubbabel and Joshua in the days of Darius I (521–486 B.C.E.), and the generation of Ezra and Nehemiah in the time of Artaxerxes I (464–424 B.C.E.). This lively tale of plots and intrigue in the court of Ahasuerus (or Xerxes I, 485–465 B.C.E.) serves primarily to describe life in exile and in royal circles, as well as to provide an aetiology of the Feast of Purim. Whenever it may have been written, by content or theme it belongs to the Persian period, as do the Chronicler's Work and other books of the Writings in their present form.

The one notable exception to this observation is the remaining book of the Writings, the Book of Daniel. It is widely agreed by scholars that, in its canonical form, this book is a product of the Greek or Hellenistic Age, dating from about 165/4 B.C.E., although it undoubtedly incorporates older materials.[4] In this respect it is different from the rest of the books in the Hebrew Bible and belongs rather with the books of the Apocrypha and other Jewish literature of the later period. Presumably it made its way into the Canon because it was perceived and believed to be a product of the sixth century, the work of the prophet Daniel who lived during the Babylonian Exile and survived into the beginning of the Persian period (cf. the chapter headings, especially 10:1, "the 3rd year of Cyrus").

I wish to set aside the Book of Daniel for the present. This book belongs with other products of the Hellenistic Age and thus constitutes a significant postscript to the Writings and the Hebrew Bible, as well as a transition to and link with a new era and a potential, if also controversial, fourth section of Scripture (now compromising the Apocrypha or Deuterocanonical books). This group of texts was accepted by many Jews, although it was ultimately refused admission to the Hebrew Canon. But it was preserved in the Greek Bible by the early church and was maintained as canonical by the Roman Catholic communion. We propose that the rest of the Writings were assembled and promulgated in the Persian period, consciously and deliberately as part of the Hebrew Bible, and we wish to submit the following data in evidence. The total number of words in the Writings is 84,006. If we subtract Daniel from the group we arrive at the following figure:

Writings	84,006
Daniel	–5,919
Net	78,087

If we now compare the figures for the different sections of the Hebrew Bible, we find the following remarkable correspondences:

Primary History A		Remaining Parts B	
I (Torah)	79,983	IIB (Latter Prophets)	71,853
IIA (Former Prophets)	69,658	III (Writings)	78,087

Subtotal (A)	149,641
Subtotal (B)	149,940
Total (without Daniel)	299,581

The correspondences among the major segments are so close, and the symmetry so exact, that it is difficult to imagine that these are the result of happenstance, or that a single mind or group of individuals was not responsible for assembling and organizing this collection of sacred works. The omission of Daniel is based entirely on the recognition of its late date, not its numerical characteristics. While it could be argued that other books in the Canon are equally late, or at least later than the Persian period or the time of Ezra and Nehemiah, those cases are arguable.[5] The case of Daniel, however, is clear-cut, decisive, and disputed only by those who have made prior theological commitments unaffected by evidence or reasonable argument.

In addition to symmetry in length (i.e., the number of words), we can also point to other features that reflect conscious selection and organization in the case of the Writings and in relation to the other units of the Hebrew Bible. In this scheme, which is a form of chiasm with the two interior parts forming a balance (IIA-Former Prophets and IIB-Latter Prophets), we expect the Writings to match the Torah. In terms of overall length, they do. Without Daniel, the Writings are slightly shorter in length than the Torah, whereas the Latter Prophets are slightly longer than the Former Prophets. Since on other grounds there are strong links between I and IIA (i.e., together they form the Primary History), combining them indicates that we should also combine the remaining pair. The results show that the first half, the Primary History, is almost identical in length to the second half, the differences being almost entirely canceled out in the combinations of parts I and IIA and of IIB and III (the final difference is much less than 1 percent, so negligible as to be ignorable). Without Daniel, there are ten books in the Writings—double the number in the Torah. While the total number of words is about the same, the difference in the number of books is largely accounted for by the Five Rolls, or *megillot*. Although written separately, these five rolls are about the same length each as a number of the Minor Prophets, which were combined in a single scroll. The minor works in the Writings, however, were not. That the number five played a significant role in the organization of the books is clear not only from the Torah (the five Books of Moses), but also from the rolls (five books, each of which was read at a major feast or other important occasion in the religious calendar) and the five divisions of the Psalter (which must somehow be correlated with the five Books of the Torah). It is less easy to explain the prominence of the number four in the case of the Prophetic Canon, but the fact that the group is carefully divided into matching units of four is sufficient to demonstrate planning and purpose on the part of the canonizers. The additional datum, as in the case of the Torah and Writings, that the two groups match up well in length, only strengthens the case for intentionality.

The total number of books in the Hebrew Bible is not without significance either. The usual count is twenty-four. Sometimes reference is made to the number of books in Greek epic poems, but the connection is remote. On the basis of statements in Josephus[6] and the arrangement in the Greek Bible, whereby Ruth is attached to Judges and Lamentations to Jeremiah (as is still the case in most English Bibles), that number is reduced to twenty-two, which is also the number of letters in the Hebrew alphabet. The use of the alphabet as an organizing principle is well known in Hebrew poetry (e.g., the numerous examples of alphabetic acrostic poems in the Psalter, Lamentations, and elsewhere). Therefore, it seems quite likely that this correlation underlies the renumbering, and that the rearrangement reflects just such an interpretation of the collection of books. Such an interest alone makes it unlikely that the arrangement in the Greek Bible is original; in any case, it is impossible to imagine that Lamentations was originally attached to the Book of Jeremiah. Clearly it is an independent, if anonymous, composition. The same is true of Ruth in relation to Judges; it is hard to imagine how or why Ruth would have been separated from Judges if it were once part of that book. It is much easier to imagine the reverse process in both cases.

If, however, we exclude the Book of Daniel from our Persian period compilation, then the total is twenty-three; interestingly, this number has some special significance in biblical numerology. It is an alternate to the twenty-two-letter count for alphabetic (and nonalphabetic) acrostics; in several cases an additional line or bicolon is appended to complete the poem. Since the twenty-third line or unit always begins with the Hebrew letter *pe*, it has been suggested that the poet embedded or incorporated yet another device in his poem—pointing to the opening, middle (twelfth line), and last lines, whose initial letters (*'aleph, lamed*, and *pe*) will form the word *'aleph*, the first letter of the alphabet and the symbol for it (just as we use a combination of the first two letters of the Greek alphabet, alpha and beta, to form our name for the whole sequence).[7] The Greek words are themselves a transparent adoption and adaptation of the Phoenician originals, which are the same as Hebrew.

It seems likely to me that the compiler of the Hebrew Bible had in mind the twenty-three-letter scheme used in numerous poems in the Bible when assembling the books. The idea was to show or affirm completion. The entire alphabet, from A to Z as we would say, is covered in the Hebrew Scriptures, and it seems to me that the twenty-third book serves precisely the role of closing out the Canon. The book of Ezra-Nehemiah not only forms an envelope with Chronicles at the beginning of the Writings, showing that it is the tenth and final work of this part of the Bible, but it also has links with the opening section, the Torah, as already shown. Ezra, toward the end of Ezra-Nehemiah, reads extensively from the Torah, thereby reaffirming the link with the past and renewing the covenant that ties Yahweh to his people and vice versa. That the intention of men like Ezra and Nehemiah was to stabilize and normalize the situation of the Jewish community seems obvious; that they would be interested in setting things in order once and for all would also fit the circumstances. It would not have been long after the events described that the Hebrew Bible of the Persian period was complete.

The intrusion or insertion of the Book of Daniel into this otherwise symmetrical arrangement of the books of the Bible only serves to show that this Canon was not yet (or ever) closed; that new crises and perils, as well as opportunities, evoke new responses and ultimately new adjustments need to be made. But behind the creative tumult of the Hellenistic-Roman age, we witness also the production of the Apocrypha (the fourth segment of the Canon) and numerous non-canonical works (as seen in the library at Qumran and in the long lists of pseudepigraphic books).[8]

As already mentioned, in the oldest and best manuscripts the Chronicler's Work serves as a frame or envelope for the Writings, with Chronicles at the beginning and Ezra-Nehemiah at the end. That this arrangement was a matter of some antiquity and significance is shown by the repetition of the last paragraph of 2 Chronicles as the first paragraph of Ezra-Nehemiah, an indication that the continuity of the books had been broken. If they were side by side, or Ezra-Nehemiah followed Chronicles directly, there would be no need or use for such a repetition. But if they were separated by a number of unrelated works, then there would be both a need and a point in resuming the work by this repetition and thus calling attention to the place at which the narrative was interrupted.[9] Hence one can say, given the present ordering of the books in question, that the only correct placement is as we have them in the best medieval manuscripts. The point of division seems to have been dictated by the fact that, since Chronicles runs parallel to the Book of Kings for most of its length, it would be appropriate to terminate the book at approximately the same place that Kings ends. Kings and Chronicles diverge at the end. Kings provides some incidental information about the accession of Evil-Merodach to the Babylonian throne after the death of his father, Nebuchadnezzar, and a kindness shown to the captive Judahite king, Jehoiachin, while Chronicles ends on a more hopeful and encouraging note with the Edict of Cyrus concerning the return of the exiles to their homeland.

In the light of this arrangement, the Chronicler's Work proves an invaluable guide to the remaining contents of the Writings, as the compiler intended. Thus, while the Chronicler's Work begins with Adam in a recapitulation of the preceding segments of the Bible starting with Genesis, the earlier part of the story is covered in barest outline by a lengthy succession of genealogies, with some annotations. Anticipating what is to follow, these genealogies highlight the two lines or dynasties that are of most interest to him and presumably to his audience: the line of Aaron (and Zadok) and the House of David, the high priesthood and the monarchy, respectively.

The story proper, however, begins with David and his accession to the throne of Judah on the death of Saul. The rest of Chronicles is devoted to the exploits and achievements of the royal house, concentrating most attention on David himself—not only as the model king, but above all on his activities in preparing for the building of the Temple, a task that will be accomplished by his illustrious son, Solomon, and in organizing the official worship and cultic practices for the Temple in Jerusalem. While extolling and elaborating on David's efforts and achievements with respect to worship in the Temple, the writer manages to overlook most of the questionable activities—intrigues, plots, murders, and the like—that make the account in 2 Samuel through 1 Kings so much more interesting and valuable as a source for what actually occurred in those days. The account in Chronicles is all the more instructive for what it omits and what it adds in revealing the compiler's preferences and biases while at the same time making clear the saintly image of David held by the faithful hundreds of years after he lived. Probably, this is the way David would have preferred to be remembered—how he was and is: anointed king of Israel, defender of the faith, model of piety and wise ruler, and founder of the only dynasty to rule in Judah from his day to the end of the kingdom. He was thus a symbol of kingship for the future. The restoration of the monarchy may have been a genuine possibility at one time; however, with fading political chances, the figure of David became an eschatological hope. Thus there arose within Jewish tradition the expectation that, at the end of time, his royal descendant, the Messiah, would emulate his distant ancestor and reestablish the ancient kingdom.

Although a much more realistic portrayal was preserved in the Primary History, in the end it was the sanitized version of Chronicles—a greatly embellished and elaborated presentation—that won the day. So David survived in story, song, and legend in the image created by the Chronicler, and that accomplishment is borne out by the other books in the Writings relating to David and his family. Much the same can be said of Solomon, the revered son of a revered father. He, too, is presented in much the same fashion; extensive coverage is devoted to his reign and major achievements in the same realm of Temple and cult, as well as Palace and throne. The picture is much the same as in Kings, but signs of trouble or difficulties in behavior and proclivities that might be subject to criticism—as in Kings where Solomon is condemned for his involvement in the false worship of his many wives—are carefully brushed away. Once again we have a paragon of wisdom and piety, a hero of tradition and legend for the ages, only slightly less imposing than his illustrious father.

For the rest, Chronicles is the history of the Davidic Dynasty. Not all of the kings are equally good or up to the standard of David and Solomon as portrayed in Chronicles. However, much more attention is given to the good ones, especially the best ones like Hezekiah and Josiah, while the bad ones are passed over quickly. Emphasis is placed on the nation, the city, the Temple, and the dynasty. There is a divine commitment to all, which guarantees continuity, stability, prosperity, and security through all the vicissitudes that a tiny nation must endure. The tone is always optimistic and upbeat, and even the terrible catastrophe of 587/6—the loss of nation, city, temple, and dynasty—can be taken in stride. As with the Latter Prophets, there is a deliberate effort to contain and reverse the effect of the great central tragedy. The Chronicler's Work does not end in captivity, but in the return, restoration, and renewal of the land and the people. The achievements are modest, and Judah is not free at the end of the story (in Ezra-Nehemiah), nor is there a Davidic king on the throne; but there is promise and hope. The return is carefully described, and the terms and tones are modulated. Just to be back, to live again in their land, to rebuild the Temple and rededicate it with a Zadokite priest presiding (Joshua) and a Davidide at the head of the civil apparatus (Zerubbabel), all under Persian authority, was confirmation of the divine commitment and assurance that they would survive and enjoy peace and a measure of prosperity again.[10]

The organizer of the Writings clearly had these themes in mind when compiling the collection and may well have been part of the Chronicler's entourage, if not the Chronicler himself. The books that follow, i.e., Psalms and Proverbs, are directly connected with the royal house and with the special interests of the founding dynasts, David and Solomon. Later tradition attributed the whole book of Psalms to David, but in the Bible a much lesser claim is made. In the Massoretic Text, seventy-three out of one hundred fifty Psalms are attributed to David, while smaller groups are attributed to others, including temple musicians and other personnel; Solomon and Moses are also credited with one each. Additionally, some headings spell out the circumstances and connections between individual Psalms and events or crises in David's life. Without attempting to judge whether any of these claims can be substantiated, we can maintain that the connections are reasonable. David's reputation as musician and composer, as well as poet, is secure; whether or not the specific associations can be demonstrated or even defended, the essential picture is correct. David was not just a warrior and politician, he was what the Bible says he was: poet, lyrist, and hymnist. The Psalms are a monument to his name and reputation.

The book is the hymnal of the Second Temple, as is often said, but it derives its contents mostly from the First Temple period. It runs the whole gamut of hymnody, from lament to praise, confession to thanksgiving, ringing all the changes of mood and tone that the human heart and mind are capable of when expressing the strongest feelings about the individual's and community's relationship to its God. Such a hymnal is a necessity for any religious community. In the case of the Bible, its intimate connection with Chronicles exhibits the linkage between Temple and hymnody and is symbolized by the name of David, who orchestrated the whole arrangement as music master of the Temple and its liturgy.[11]

With the Book of Proverbs, the relationship to Solomon is just as intimate and symbolic as is Psalms with David. While Solomon is credited with most of the sayings in the book, some are attributed to others. Overall, we can recognize that much of the content is simply popular wisdom of the ancient world, albeit formulated in distinctive Hebraic terms and tones. That Solomon had a reputation for wisdom is certain, and he may well have been wise and said some of the things attributed to him. That he sponsored a school of sorts for his own children and those of palace personnel may be taken for granted. Certainly it would have been both a prerogative and a responsibility of the monarchy to do so, and the book may well be a product of a school like that and the experience of teachers and students. It is clear that any society, especially a monarchy, will have such teachings, and these are associated with one of the most successful monarchs of his time and place. The tone is appropriate as well, since the mood is generally upbeat and stable, and the advice is highly practical. In addition, the objective is clear: to maintain law and order, traditional hierarchical relationships, and to encourage piety and decency—essentially a primer or reader on what the covenant obligations mean in daily living and how to get on successfully in the social order.[12] The assumptions and presuppositions of the Chronicler are clearly present, though the exact relationship may be hard to define or explain. Suffice it to say that the compiler or organizer was fully in tune with both compositions, and he saw Proverbs, along with Psalms, as supplementary and complementary to the Chronicler's Work.

Passing by Job, which requires special attention, we turn to the *megillot*, or Five Rolls. The first three—Ruth, Song of Songs, and Ecclesiastes—clearly fit into the framework we have established for the Writings. The Book of Ruth is an idyllic story set in the period of the Judges. Because its title character is a Moabite woman who becomes a wife and mother in Israel, it has often been interpreted as a plea for tolerance against the draconian ethnocentric rules laid down by Ezra and enforced by Nehemiah.[13] While such an interpretation of the text is possible, it is not likely that this was the intention or interest of the author, who seems rather to have written up the tradition because it concerned a direct ancestor of David; Ruth and Boaz were his great-grandparents. The fact that both of them in their lives and actions embodied the highest principles and ideals of Israelite life would not be lost on any reader, and so this bit of family tradition, duly enhanced and polished by high literary art, entered the permanent records of God's people. In turn, it may be noted that Boaz was the grandson of Nahshon, the leader of the tribe of Judah during the generation of the Exodus (cf. Numbers 2:7). Verifiable or not, the widely accepted view was that David came of good stock, inheriting leadership qualities from a rich array of ancestors.

Both the Song of Songs and Ecclesiastes are attributed to Solomon, and traditionally are assigned to widely separated periods of his life: Song of Songs to celebrate a wedding presumably when he was in the prime of life and Ecclesiastes when he was an old man, ruminating and reflecting on his wide range of experiences.[14] While there is a great deal of controversy over the content and meaning of Song of Songs—apart from its patently erotic character, just what it is about, how many people are involved, and especially how a collection of love songs managed to get into the Bible—I think we can give some straightforward answers to some basic questions. From the heading, it is clear that the editor believed that Solomon composed the book, or at least that the poems were connected with him and dedicated to him. The occasion is spelled out in the book itself, which refers to a formal solemn wedding between Solomon and presumably the female lead or heroine of the book (cf. Song of Songs 3:11—"Go forth and look, O daughters of Zion, at King Solomon with the crown with which his mother crowned him on the day of his wedding, on the day of his heart's rejoicing"). The association with Solomon would have sufficed to allay concerns and qualify this assemblage of ornately decorative poetry for inclusion in the Canon. Later generations of rabbis and church fathers would wrestle with problems of plain meaning and possible deeper theological significance, finally saving the book for future generations of the faithful by allegorizing the principal parties and their behavior. The best that can be said is that official Jewish and Christian interpretations are about equidistant from the plain meaning of the passages in question.

With regard to Ecclesiastes, similar questions have been raised, chiefly because of the skeptical pessimistic tone of the book. It reads to a considerable extent as a kind of counterweight to the positive tone of Proverbs and its confident air about traditional morality and ethical behavior, or as a kind of antiestablishment tract, taking aim at standard Deuteronomic theology. Still, in its present form, more conventional admonitions occur here and there to neutralize some of the more dramatic challenges to traditional faith. While the king repeats the familiar motto of the book, "Vanity of vanities . . . all is vanity," he also is quoted as saying, "Fear God and keep his commandments! For this is the whole duty of humanity. Indeed, every work God will bring into judgment . . . whether for good or for evil" (12:13). Doubtless the reference to the king, son of David, in the heading counted heavily in the final assessment of the book. While Solomon is not named directly, it is hard to imagine that the editor/compiler had anyone else in mind, although conceivably the title could apply to other kings descended from David. But, apart from David, only Solomon actually ruled over Israel from Jerusalem. Whatever their claims or titles, after Solomon only Judah remained under their sway.

The other rolls of the *megillot* are not directly related to the major themes of the Chronicler, or to the House of David, but considering their credentials, they could hardly have been excluded. The first is the Book of Lamentations, which may seem a little out of place in the context of the Chronicler's Work with its optimistic view of Judah's history. While the Chronicler can hardly overlook the Fall of Jerusalem and while he dutifully copies his source in Kings, he hastens to emphasize that all such events are only temporary setbacks, that the end of the exile and the return to the land and the rebuilding of city and temple are at hand. The Book of Lamentations, on the contrary, comes directly out of the terrible tragedy. It expresses the mood of appalling sorrow, alternating between indignation and resignation, but clearly evoking the grim and bitter experience with supreme artistry and skill. It belongs rather with the Primary History and especially the Book of Jeremiah, to which it has been attached in different canonical traditions. Nevertheless, it is an independent work, associated with the observance of the Ninth of Ab (the date of the destruction of Jerusalem in 587/6), a melancholy event reinforced in postbiblical times by the coincidental destruction of the city and the Temple of Herod on the same date in 70 C.E. Lamentations may strike a slightly jarring note in the Writings, but a necessary and important one. As with the Primary History and the Latter Prophets, the theme of tragedy is present always as a possibility, often as a reality, and can only be overcome by the supervening grace of an ultimately compassionate deity.

The remaining roll is the Book of Esther, which provides an interlude between the events mentioned in the Chronicler's Work—after the initial return and reconstruction of the Temple under the leadership of Zerubbabel of the House of David and Joshua the Zadokite High Priest, during the reign of Darius I, and before the return of Ezra and Nehemiah to institute reforms and carry out divine and royal mandates during the reign of Artaxerxes I.[15] In Esther, the king is Ahasuerus (Xerxes I), and the events belong more to the realm of legend than history. In the end, after a certain amount of terror and suspense, it is a happy episode for the Jews who remained behind in the eastern regions of the Persian Empire rather than returning to their homeland. Their success is celebrated in festive fashion, thereby creating a precedent and establishing a new feast on the Jewish calendar, one that has proved durable and immensely popular over the centuries. If only because it provides an explanation and rationale for the Feast of Purim, the book would have to be retained, and so it has been. Besides, it served to lift the spirits, especially when read after the unrelieved tragedy of Lamentations, and offered encouragement and hope to those living in exile (although of their own will). Like the stories in Daniel, it emphasizes the importance of constancy in religion and devotion and observance of the rules, but above all loyalty and faithfulness to fellow Jews. The theme of divine protection and deliverance in crises is present but concealed in the strictly human level of activity, and in the lack of an overt mention of or appeal to the Deity.

Excluding the Book of Daniel, this collection of three poetic books (Psalms, Proverbs, Job) and five scrolls (Ruth, Song of Songs, Ecclesiastes, Lamentations, and Esther) is found between the two (unequal) parts of the Chronicler's Work. The Chronicler has reshaped the story of Judah and its kings substantially. By eliminating the Northern Kingdom almost entirely from his work, he has focussed attention on Judah, Jerusalem, the Temple, and the dynasty of David, where in his view the divine choice has been set and where the future of his kingdom and his people lies. Now in the story continuing beyond the range of Kings, in Ezra-Nehemiah, the Chronicler reports the Edict of Cyrus, the return from exile, the rebuilding and rededication of the Temple, and the revival of community life in the ancient homeland. All this is presented as confirmation of his understanding of the divine commitment to his people and his confidence in a national future. It is also presented as a vindication of the prophets who faithfully transmitted the word of God—both the good and the bad news— but who were convinced that destruction and disaster were never a final word, only a necessary punishment and prelude to a new era of restoration and revival.

In phase one of the return, the events were sufficiently dramatic and substantive to lend hope for a national revival—full restoration of the kingdom under the rule of a legitimate king (of the House of David) and high priest (of the Zadokite line). The high-water mark was reached with the rededication of the newly refurbished Temple in the sixth year of Darius I (516/15 B.C.E.). What, if anything, happened after that is unclear. There is a gap in the reports, but while the high priests continued in a straight line for several centuries, we hear no more about the House of David and the civil rule in Jerusalem.[16] While the line continues and 1 Chronicles 3 preserves the list of descendants down into the fifth century, perhaps to the end of it, none of those mentioned seems to have served as governor or in a leadership role. When Nehemiah takes over as governor, it is strictly as a representative of the Persian government, of which he was an important official. He is a faithful, loyal, pious Jew, but without the royal claims or prerogatives belonging to the House of David.

It is with the second phase, the age of Ezra and Nehemiah, who lived and carried out their missions in the reign of Artaxerxes

I (464–424), that our story and that of the Writings come to a close (with the exception of Daniel, which will be discussed separately). In many ways, Ezra is the key figure in both stories. For a number of converging reasons, it is widely held by scholars that the editor of the Chronicler's Work and the author of the Ezra Memoirs in Ezra-Nehemiah (Ezra, chaps. 7–10) are the same person.[17] I subscribe to this view and believe that Ezra was responsible for the present form of the Chronicler's Work from the beginning of 1 Chronicles through Ezra 6, which concludes the account of the rebuilding and rededication of the Temple. Included is an excursus on the search of the records in the royal archives, a search that carries down to the reign of Artaxerxes I, or the time of Ezra himself, so that part of the work could not have been completed any earlier than that time. Ezra also kept a diary or wrote his own memoirs about events and achievements in his own time. This was a separate work, as the gap (of about sixty years) between Ezra 6 and 7 makes clear. His ultimate intention may have been to continue the Chronicler's Work from 515 B.C.E. and the Temple story down to his own time, using records available to him or to which he had access, as well as his own memoirs. In any event, he never achieved this objective, and no one else did either. It is reasonable to suppose that he died before completing (or perhaps consolidating) either work, if that was his intention.

The task of compilation and publication devolved on Nehemiah, the governor and colleague of Ezra, who apparently outlived the latter. Nehemiah, in the meantime, had written or was writing his own memoirs, recording his activities as ambassador of the king and governor of the province, and these are now to be found in the surviving books of Ezra-Nehemiah. Being a busy official and administrator—and as his memoirs show, not being a literary person or a practiced editor—he did the least possible tampering with the material at hand, and just combined and consolidated the Chronicler's Work with the memoirs of Ezra and his own. Since the two latter works overlapped and intersected at several points, he may have tried to interweave them in order to provide a consecutive account of events. In the process, he may also have confused matters, but it now appears that the two sets of memoirs have been interwoven, and it is not always easy to determine the precise course of events or how the parts relate to each other. In any case, Nehemiah closed with his own last words and thus completed the task begun much earlier, but undertaken in his own time by Ezra to cap the Hebrew Bible. With the closing of the Chronicler's Work, we also come to the end of the Writings, and, in the same way, to the conclusion of the Hebrew Bible. It may be pure coincidence that the Book of Genesis begins with the words *běrē'šît . . . 'ĕlōhîm,* "In the beginning, . . . God . . . ," while the book of Ezra-Nehemiah ends with the words *'ĕlōhay lĕṭôbâ,* ". . . my God for good." We need not point out that "good" is the theme word of Genesis 1:1–2:3, and remains the leitmotif of the whole Hebrew Bible. It is also possible that Nehemiah turned the task over to an anonymous assistant, who, true to his task, has remained unknown, the invisible editor, to this day.

The closing date for all of this activity should occur during the time Nehemiah was still alive and not long after the events recorded in his memoirs. The latest reference (Nehemiah 12:22), which remains somewhat obscure, is to Darius the Persian.[18] In context, this person can hardly be the great Darius I of the previous century; he is much more likely to be Darius II (424–405), the son and successor of Artaxerxes I. Thus a date in the reign of this Darius, perhaps about 420, would be entirely appropriate.

The Book of Job is something of an anomaly in the Hebrew Bible. Not only is it in the form of a poetic thematic dialogue, sandwiched between a prose introduction and an epilogue, but it raises serious questions about divine governance of the world of human beings.[19] Job, the innocent victim of a wager between God and The Adversary (*haśśāṭān*), complains so vociferously about the unfair treatment meted out to him and criticizes divine justice and fairness so vehemently, that God himself is drawn into the debate between Job and his friends. The friends defend traditional piety and the basic and prevailing biblical stance regarding the morality of the universe—the fundamental dictum that God is just and that people finally, if not immediately, get what they deserve or better because God is not only just, but kind and merciful; Job, however, argues with greater skill and success that the opposite is true.[20]

Because the reader knows more about the situation than any of the human participants, he or she can tell that Job has the stronger case—his suffering is uncalled for and reflects badly on the principle of divine justice; finally, a response from God himself is needed. The principal argument of the Voice from the Whirlwind is that Job is not speaking out of knowledge and wisdom, but from limited experience; he cannot begin to understand the complexity of the universe being manipulated by God, let alone human existence itself. The dialogue ends with Job's repentance and recantation. While the book closes in fairy-tale fashion with the restoration of Job to his former state and the restoration of his lost possessions—with additional ample compensation for his pain and suffering—the basic agonizing question remains to be answered.

How does Job fit into the larger context of the Canon, especially in relation to the major narratives and teachings of the Bible? If we take the book as a whole, and that is the way the editors of the book and of the Bible wished it to be understood, then we must admit that it fits in quite well. In the end, Job affirms and confirms the basic biblical doctrine of divine justice. Whatever trials and tribulations he undergoes, in the end Job is not only restored but compensated for his ordeal. One major lesson of the book is that in spite of serious questions about the operation of divine justice and the corresponding attribute of mercy—and the considerable evidence to the contrary that Job adduces and that human experience confirms—the conclusion drawn is that God rules over nature and humanity and that he is just and kind as the Prologue, Epilogue, and the Voice from the Whirlwind attest. There are difficulties and complexities in the entire operation, however, that make things seem or be otherwise; besides, it is all beyond the grasp of the human intellect. Thus the editors reaffirm the basic principles of biblical religion. At the same time, they allow for exceptions, even contradictions, and attempt to put everything into a larger and more complex framework—appealing at once to the God of creation and ancient Canaanite myth (El) and to the God of the covenant of justice and mercy (Yahweh). So Job deepens and broadens the theology of the Bible, challenging human beings to reach beyond the simplistic morality of traditional religion to a more sophisticated and nuanced theology—one that embraces the universe ruled by God, but in which humanity occupies a subordinant place, subject to forces or factors not only beyond our control but even our comprehension. In this way the concerns of the Israelites arising out of their mixed and traumatic experience are put into a much larger setting and thought-frame— one rooted in the great myths of the past and here brought into contact with the Israelite experience so that the two are amalgamated, forming a universal faith able to assimilate the epic experiences of Israel's past, to cope with present reality, and to face the possibilities of the future.

The Book of Daniel remains outside the loop.[21] Perhaps some of the others do, as well, but it is strikingly the case with this book. Since its date (in its present form, because doubtless it incorporates some older sources) is much later than any of the other books of the Hebrew Bible, and since it clearly does not belong to the framework of the Chronicler's Work or any of the other Writings, it must be treated in a separate category.

What its presence in the Canon shows, first of all, is that whatever the rationale for its inclusion (and its presumed or inferred date in the sixth century would be a prime consideration), the Canon was not closed; it was possible to include books of recent vintage so long as a plausible case could be made for their inspiration, authority, and early date.

In the second place, its presence serves as a warning that in another sense the Canon is never closed, because new situations produce new crises for the people of God, and existing norms and standards cannot stand in place of new revelation and understanding of the will of God. Reading the Book of Daniel brings us into a world far different from that of the stable, settled province of the Persian Empire of the sixth to fifth century. With all the threats from hostile neighbors, and dissident and recalcitrant members within the community, the situation of Judah in the days of Ezra-Nehemiah—as also in the days of Zerubbabel and Joshua—was essentially secure and peaceful, and for two hundred years or so that basic stability was maintained.

The world of Daniel both in stories and visions is fraught with peril, personal and corporate, and only the most consistent faith and utter trust will bring a person through. The times are so threatening that only direct action by Almighty God can rectify a situation in which pagan tyrants rule with a vengeful and persecuting hand, defy the Lord God himself, desecrate his sanctuary, and erect an image of their own false god in the Holy Place of worship. For such a crisis, a new *Gattung*, or a new form of literature, was required, one based on the earlier prophetic visions of the end time when the old world would collapse in destructive violence and be replaced by a new earth—even a new heavens in which there would be a final climactic struggle between the forces of good and evil. In the end, a new order and a new era would emerge: the reign of God himself over his faithful survivors. In this framework of a final judgment by God on a sinful world, the dead will also play their part—the faithful to be raised to eternal life, the wicked to suffer everlasting torment. With Daniel, we enter into the world of apocalyptic visions, coded messages, revelations through dreams, and angelic interpreters.[22] The message of the book is to be faithful, even to death, in the face of pagan persecution. The stories in Daniel testify to the power of God to save those who are loyal and devoted to him and who resist both temptation and testing. While the stories have happy endings, it was recognized that what counted was not so much the outcome as the courage and conviction of the martyrs, a tradition that has been extended and amplified through centuries of persecution.

The visions, for their part, portray the end of the present evil age and its replacement by God's own kingdom wherein the saints will find release from their suffering and new eternal life in a permanent paradise. It would take a major essay to delve into the details of this new literature, which is rooted in prophetic visions of the past, but incorporates fresh ideas from a multitude of sources belonging to the world of Hellenism, dualism, astrology, religious politics involving the king as deity or his surrogate, and much more. To properly analyze and evaluate a book like Daniel, we need to study it in the context of contemporary sacred literature, e.g., the so-called Apocrypha and/or Pseudepigrapha. Many of these books achieved canonical status among certain groups of Jews, at least for a while, a status preserved in the Greek Bible and affirmed in the Roman Catholic Church to this day. In other words, books such as Maccabees (1 and 2), Esdras (1 and 2), Judith, Tobit, Wisdom, and the rest, are worthy companions of Daniel—not to speak of the authoritative literature of Qumran, which shares many features with Daniel—and served as guides for the community.[23] The New Testament, the sacred literature (along with the Old Testament) of the Christian Church, not only made extensive use of Daniel itself, but shares features and characteristics with it. In the Book of Revelation, we have a dramatic counterpart from a period about 250 years later. In addition to common themes and objectives, there are important affinities, beyond vocabulary and imagery, which they share, and one might argue that together these two books seem to form a frame around the apocalyptic era.

It is important to note that Daniel is very much a part of the Hebrew Bible, accepted along with the other books. While its credentials may have been misleading, its contents were taken at face value and accepted by the faithful. So there is a significant part of the Hebrew Bible that reaches beyond the confines of the Persian period and the setting of Ezra-Nehemiah into the maelstrom of the Hellenistic world, with its bombardment of Greek culture and philosophy, the intrusion of pagan religion, and the overwhelming impact of political-military leaders in the fragments of Alexander's Empire. The Bible was not left to itself, but was brought into this new world, which required and received new responses. The Book of Daniel reveals and reflects both that world and the reactions given by loyal Jews. Out of that matrix came new movements and activities and a vast literature that only succeeding centuries could and would sort out. The Hebrew Bible was thus embarked on a perilous course, the end of which could hardly be foreseen. During the same period, other books would be attached to the Jewish Bible, and other developments would ensue. Daniel belongs to the Hebrew Bible, but with additions it also belongs to the Greek Bible and the literature of Qumran, and finally had an important impact on the New Testament as well.[24]

Conclusion

In this monograph, I have presented a case for the unity of the Hebrew Bible—as a literary composite. Certainly there can be no argument for unitary authorship, since different parts and books arise from vastly different times and places. But we can speak about compilation and organization, what we mean by editing or redacting in the broad sense. From a study of the Bible's contents, style, language, and literary features, I conclude that there is a pervasive unity, elements that tie individual components into a complex but unified structure. Thus we can divide the Hebrew Bible roughly in half, each half consisting of two major parts. The first half consists of the largest unit in the Hebrew Bible, the Primary History, extending over nine books and containing 150,000 words, almost half of the total of 305,500. This work is a product of the Babylonian period (mid-sixth century), although it is a composite of older sources, some much older. This is the basic official story of Israel from its very beginning to the dismal end of the national entity—with military defeat, loss of the land, and captivity of the people. The message is essentially twofold. First, God created the people Israel and sustained them because of his promise to the fathers. Second, because they failed to live up to the terms of the agreement or covenant, God punished them, and now they have lost everything. Nevertheless, there is always a chance for the future, but it depends on their learning the lesson of repentance and renewed fidelity to their God.

The remaining parts of the Hebrew Bible, the Latter Prophets and the Writings, are products of a later period. The Latter Prophets are from the Persian era, perhaps late sixth or early fifth century; the Writings come mostly (and in an organized fashion) from the time and hands of that odd couple, Ezra and Nehemiah. In addition, there is the Book of Daniel, a product of the Greek period (about 165 B.C.E.).

The Latter Prophets offer a corrective or balance for the Primary History. In this collection, the Major and Minor Prophets are represented; they had something to say about the central catastrophic event, the Fall of Jerusalem, or about what led to it or away from it, i.e., the preceding century and the decades following the fall of the city. First of all, there is a strong affirmation of the Primary History and its message of judgment and punishment. There is also, however, an equally strong or stronger message of hope and comfort. The Latter Prophets go beyond the Primary History and portray the end of the exile and the return and restoration of the community, along with the rebuilding of the Temple. The result is that people and confidence are restored, and while hoping for something better, they can be content with their current lot and confirmed in their belief in the power of God and his intervention in their behalf.

The Writings offer further confirmation and support for their views. The Chronicler's Work, which encompasses the Writings, retells the story of the Primary History, but with a different perspective and many changes in details. It emphasizes especially the kingdom of Judah, which survived in the preservation of the province of *Yehud* under Persian rule and protection. It also focuses attention on the city of Jerusalem, the dynasty of David, and the permanence of Yahweh's commitment to his people. The story is brought up to the time of Ezra-Nehemiah, extending well beyond the Primary History, and balancing the tragedy of the fall of the nation and city with its partial restoration and recovery. The message is essentially the same as that of the Latter Prophets. In place of a tragic ending there is a new beginning, but as Ezra and Nehemiah make clear, the rules are the same and the possibilities are for either good or bad results. Faithfulness and loyal obedience to God and his commandments are required, while deviations and violations will be dealt with sternly. However, faithfulness will be rewarded, although the immediate prospect is for survival and continuity, rather than fulfillment of promise and success.

The Book of Daniel belongs to a different genre, a different spirit, and a different age. It opens up a whole new Hellenistic world of apocalyptic visions and end-of-the-age forecasts. This takes us into the additional literature of the Greek Bible, and from there into the vast ferment of the Greco-Roman era, which saw the emergence of new groups within Judaism with their own sacred literature, including the sectaries of Qumran and the Christian community with its New Testament.

Notes

Prepared by John R. Huddlestun

Lecture 1

1. Our dating of the event follows the older traditional chronology of 458 B.C.E. for Ezra's return under the Persian king Artaxerxes I (465–424 B.C.E.). For discussion and the chronological options, see, e.g., Rowley 1965, 137–68; Widengren in Hayes and Miller 1977, 503–9; and Bright 1981, 391–402.

Exactly what this "Book of the Law of Moses" (Hebrew *sēpher tôrat mošeh*, Nehemiah 8:1) comprised remains a much discussed question in biblical scholarship. Tradition has identified the document with some form of our present Pentateuch (Torah), and the majority of modern scholars are inclined to agree that—at the very least—portions of Pentateuchal law were involved. For discussion and bibliography, see Kellermann 1968; Houtman 1981; Williamson 1985, xxxvii–xxxix, and 1987, 90–98; and Blenkinsopp 1988, 152–7.

2. The version or publication of the Hebrew Scriptures (Old Testament) referred to in these lectures is the one most commonly used by biblical scholars: *Biblia Hebraica Stuttgartensia,* ed. K. Elliger and W. Rudolph (Stuttgart: Deutsche Bibelstiftung, 1977). All translations are those of the author. A reliable and up-to-date translation of the Hebrew Bible may be found in the most recently revised version produced by the Jewish Publication Society: *Tanakh: A New Translation of* The Holy Scriptures *According to the Traditional Hebrew Text* (Philadelphia: The Jewish Publication Society, 1985).

All word counts (following the Hebrew text) are based on the work of F. I. Andersen and A. D. Forbes (see pp. 165–83 in Meyers and O'Connor 1983 for preliminary publication).

3. Apparently, the first scholar—aside from the initial compiler(s)—to have isolated these nine books as a narrative unit was the seventeenth-century Jewish philosopher Baruch Spinoza, in his *Tractatus theologico-politicus*, first published anonymously in 1670. Spinoza attributed their compilation and in some cases composition to Ezra the Scribe; see the somewhat dated translation in *The Chief Works of Benedict de Spinoza*, vol. 1, ed. and trans. R. H. M. Elwes (New York: Dover Publications, 1951 [reprinted from the 1883 edition], 120–33. An authoritative translation of the tractate is forthcoming in Edwin Curley's *The Collected Works of Spinoza*, vol. 2, Princeton University Press.

More recently, a similar view of these books was proposed by Gustav Hölscher (among others), who believed that Genesis through 2 Kings formed "in reality a single, connected work that was only later divided into nine separate books" (Hölscher 1952, 7–8). For the first use of the term *Primary History*, see Freedman 1962 and 1963. Useful treatments of the history of scholarship on these books may be found in Hayes 1979, 156–237; Knight and Tucker 1985, 263–305; and Whybray 1987, 17–219.

4. Ever since the demise (or nearly so) of the so-called Biblical Theology Movement with its espousal of the uniqueness of the biblical writer's view of history (see, e.g., Childs 1970), biblical scholars have again struggled to define precisely how and when Israelite historiography emerged within its ancient Near Eastern context. Two of the most recent offerings in this regard—representative, to be sure, of differing perspectives—are Van Seters 1983 and Halpern 1988. (On the former, note the review of Z. Zevit in *BASOR* 260 [1985], 71–82.)

5. See Freedman 1989, 31.

6. For discussion of the Decalogue (and further bibliography), see Stamm and Andrew 1967; Phillips 1970; Greenberg 1971; Childs 1974, 385–439; Segal and Levi 1990; Weinfeld 1990; and Brooks 1990 (in Rabbinic tradition).

7. In the mid- to late-nineteenth century, but with antecedents reaching as far back as the early eighteenth, biblical scholars were able to identify and isolate individual literary sources employed in the composition of our present day Pentateuch. These postulated "documentary" sources, whether indicative of individuals or schools, were (and still are) commonly referred to (following the traditional chronological order) as J (Jahwist), E (Elohist), D (the Deuteronomic source, comprising the bulk of Deuteronomy), and P (the Priestly source). However, biblical scholars today disagree over virtually every issue related to the study of these

sources, with some doubting their very existence. For orientation to this four-source theory and its colorful history within biblical scholarship, see, e.g., Freedman 1962; Clements 1976, 7–50; Hayes 1979, 106–20 and 155–97; Knight 1983, 21–60; Knight and Tucker 1985, 263–96; Rogerson 1985; Soggin 1989, 91–121 and 150–63; and especially the more popular work of Friedman (1987), who defends the hypothesis, albeit with a few new twists. Of particular interest is the work of Tigay (see Tigay 1975 and 1985), who demonstrates, through comparative analysis with other ancient Near Eastern texts, that the existence and redactional compilation of such sources is not unique to the biblical corpus.

As for the P(riestly)-Work (for our purposes, the final form of Genesis through Numbers), scholars have long debated whether or not the priestly contribution constituted an originally independent narrative that was later combined with other traditions—the so-called JE complex (so Noth 1972 [1948], 8–19 and 228–51)—or was simply a redactional stage in the shaping of these already existing traditions (e.g., Cross 1973, 293–325; Rendtorff 1977, 141–42, 158–63). Thompson (1970) provides a detailed history of the P source in scholarship (the date of P is discussed in note 3 of lecture 2). For the D-Work, see note 15 below.

8. A portion of the material relating to the nine commandments and their violation within the Primary History was presented earlier in Freedman 1989. In their endless quest for the meaning of the text, the Rabbis may have seen something of this violation scheme (although certainly not to the extend advocated here) in their discussion of the Hebrew title (and first word) of the book of Lamentations (Hebrew 'ykh). The numerical value of each letter of this Hebrew word (1, 10, 20, and 5, respectively) was related (with a slight variation in order) to a specific event in Israel's history, which eventually resulted in her exile: "They inquired of (Simeon) ben-Azzai, saying to him, 'Expound for us the significance of this word from the book of Lamentations.' He responded, 'The people of Israel did not go into exile until they had denied (the following): the *oneness* of the Eternal One (God), the rite of circumcision given after *twenty* generations, the *Ten* Commandments, and the *five* books of the Torah.' They responded, 'From where (do you get this interpretation)?' He answered, '(From the letters of the word) 'ykh'" (translation by John Huddlestun). For the text (Hebrew and Yiddish), see S. Dunsky, *Midrash Rabbah, Echah (Lamentations)* (Montreal: Northern Printing and Lithographic Co., 1956), 101.

9. On the varying orders and enumeration of the commandments, see Nielsen 1968, 10–13; Greenberg 1971, 1439–1440; Freedman 1989, 35; Weinfeld 1990, 12–14; and White 1990, 202. For numbers 6–8, see especially Freund 1989.

10. Note in this regard the work of A. Phillips (1970), who argues that the Decalogue at Sinai represented Israel's pre-exilic criminal (as opposed to civil) law code, and as such constituted the essential element in the people's covenant with Yahweh. Thus, as a matter of criminal law and in order to insure Yahweh's continued favor, the community as a rule imposed the death penalty for any violation of the commandments. This thesis leads to some interesting and at times quite provocative interpretations of the Decalogue, many of which are relevant to this lecture. However, while there are points of contact between Phillips and certain ideas presented here, the important differences (e.g., with respect to the last commandment) will become apparent as this lecture progresses. Note Phillips's more recent restatement of his thesis and response to critics in "The Decalogue—Ancient Israel's Criminal Law," *Journal of Jewish Studies* 34 (1983): 1–20.

11. For the Nash Papyrus, a second century B.C.E. fragment containing the Decalogue and a portion of the *Shema,* see the original publication of S. A. Cook in *Proceedings of the Society of Biblical Archaeology* 25 (1903), 34–56 and M. Greenberg's entry in *Encyclopedia Judaica,* vol. 12, col. 833. The Decalogue is also preserved on one of the Deuteronomy manuscripts from Qumran (see White 1990).

For Philo, see his *On The Decalogue (De Decalogo)* X.35–37 and XII.50–51, in *Philo* vol. VII, trans. F. H. Colson, Loeb Classical Library (Cambridge, Mass.: Harvard University Press, 1937), 24–25, 32–33.

12. On Baruch ben-Neriah and the Deuteronomistic History, see further pages 47, 70–71, and note 5 of lecture 2.

13. In the Greek version (the Septuagint) and in most English-language Bibles, the Book of Ruth is placed between Judges and 1 Samuel. This insertion reflects, however, secondary and derivative associations. In the Hebrew Canon, Ruth is part of the so-called Five Rolls or *megillot:* Ruth, Song of Songs, Ecclesiastes, Lamentations, and Esther. These books form a subdivision of the third section of the Canon, the Writings, which is discussed in lecture 3 (see Campbell 1975, 33–36 and Sasson 1979, 11–12).

14. The Hebrew verbs are discussed in Moran 1967 and Childs 1974, 425–28. For *ḥmd* in particular, see especially B. Jackson's "Liability for Mere Intention in Early Jewish Law" in his *Essays in Jewish and Comparative Legal History* (Leiden: Brill, 1975), 202–34.

15. The first scholar to recognize (in publication) these five books—Deuteronomy through 2 Kings—as a unified narrative with its own particular theme(s) was Martin Noth in his 1943 work on the Deuteronomistic History (see Noth 1981 and 1987 for English translation). (While others such as Engnell and Jepsen had independently arrived at similar views,

Noth's work became, and indeed remains, the standard reference point for further discussion.) The name *Deuteronomistic History*, referred to in these lectures as the D-Work, derives from the fact that the four books of Joshua through Kings reflect (particularly from a linguistic standpoint) much of the ideology of the book of Deuteronomy itself (see Weinfeld 1972, 1–58, 320–59). For reactions to and/or modifications of Noth's original proposal, see (from among innumerable examples) von Rad 1966 (1947), 205–21; Wolff 1961; Eissfeldt 1965, 241–48; Smend 1971; Dietrich 1972; Radjawane 1973–74; Cross 1974, 274–89; Freedman 1976b; Hoffmann 1980; Friedman 1981; Nelson 1981; Peckham 1985; Provan 1988; Halpern 1988; and O'Brien 1989.

Lecture 2

1. For a general account of the history of this period (the fall of Judah, the Babylonian Exile, and the Persian period of return), see the appropriate sections within the standard surveys of Ackroyd 1968; Bright 1981; Hermann 1981; Hayes and Miller 1977; and most recently, Miller and Hayes 1986. For the exile in particular, see also Klein 1979; Newsome 1979; and the more recent sociological analysis of Smith 1989. A collection of detailed essays on the Persian period may be found in Davies and Finkelstein 1984.

As previously discussed, this period of defeat, destruction, exile, and subsequent return—essentially the sixth century B.C.E.—provided the catalyst for the collection and/or composition of much of what now constitutes the Hebrew Bible (see also Freedman 1975, 1983a, and 1990; the latter two articles introduce in condensed form a number of the major ideas presented here).

On the prophetic books in particular and their historical context, see Gottwald 1964 and Blenkinsopp 1983. Over the past decade or so, biblical scholars have increasingly recognized the value of sociological and anthropological studies as important aids in understanding the phenomenon of biblical prophecy (see especially Wilson 1980 and Overholt 1989).

2. For these two works, see also notes 7 and 15 to lecture 1. The traditional view of a unified "Priestly School/Source" with the so-called Holiness Code (Leviticus 17–26) as its earliest stratum has been challenged recently by I. Knohl, who questions the idea of "two major theological trends in the Torah literature, Priestly and Deuteronomistic" (1987, 67). Instead, Knohl attempts to demonstrate that P actually "constitute[s] two distinct streams with sharply differing theological and ritual conceptions" (66). These two streams are the "Priestly Torah" and the "Holiness School," the latter of which, according to Knohl, is the latest and responsible for the final recension of the former.

3. For various reasons (especially linguistic), a number of scholars now tend to date P's work (or portions of it) earlier (e.g., early exilic or pre-exilic period) than has traditionally been the case (see Hurvitz 1974, 1982, and 1988; Polzin 1976; Rendsburg 1980; Haran 1981; Zevit 1982; and Friedman 1981, 1987). For the traditional view (exilic and/or post-exilic in date), see, e.g., Wellhausen 1885, 1–51 passim; Driver 1913, 135–43; Eissfeldt 1965: 204–9; Vink 1969; and Cross 1973, 323–25.

4. Particularly with the work of the Norwegian scholar Sigmund Mowinckel (in 1914), scholars have noted and discussed the presence of Deuteronomistic language (language characteristic of the D-Work) in various prose sermons of the Book of Jeremiah. This language has often been explained as the result of Deuteronomistic editorial activity (especially in the work of W. Thiel), but scholars are—and probably will remain—divided over this issue (see Weinfeld 1972, 27–32; the essays of Cazelles, Hyatt, Holladay, and McKane in Perdue and Kovacs 1984; and the summary cf scholarship in Carroll 1986, 38–50; McKane 1986, xli–l; and Holladay 1986–89, 2:53–64).

The linguistic relationship between Ezekiel and P is admirably treated in Hurvitz 1982.

5. The ascription of authorship of the D-Work to Baruch (and his small group) places less emphasis—if any at all—on the role of Jeremiah as discussed by R. E. Friedman (1987, 147). For varying estimations of the role of Baruch, see, e.g., Muilenburg 1970; Carroll 1986, 44–45, 61; and Dearman 1990.

6. This idea of the D-group in Egypt and P-group in Babylon follows R. E. Friedman (see his essay in Halpern and Levenson 1981, 191; see also Freedman 1983a, 171). Possible evidence for communication between the two groups is found in Jeremiah 51:59–64, where Seriah, Baruch's brother, escorts the Judean king Zedekiah to Babylon. Before leaving, Seraiah is given a copy of Jeremiah's oracles concerning Babylon (=Jeremiah 50:1–51:58?) and is commanded by the prophet to read them to the Babylonian exiles (this reading follows the preserved Hebrew text, as opposed to the Septuagint, which contains a number of significant changes and/or additions; see Holladay 1986–89, 2:432–35).

The impetus for the collection or codification of Jewish legal tradition(s) during this period may relate to—or at least is illuminated by—a decree issued under Darius I (in his fourth year, 518 B.C.E.), wherein the satrap of Egypt is instructed to gather "the wise men among the soldiers, priests and scribes of Egypt" to assist in codifying local Egyptian law. When completed, this collection (translated into Aramaic and Demotic) became a valuable aid to the Persian satrap in his administration of Egypt (see E. Bresciani in *Cambridge History of Iran*, vol. II. [Cambridge: Cambridge University Press, 1985], 507–8). The implications of this for Ezra's mission under Persian rule have, of course, not gone unnoticed by biblical scholars (e.g., de Vaux 1971, 73–79; Widengren in Hayes and Miller 1977, 515; and Bickerman 1989, 30–31).

7. The relationship between Chronicles and Ezra-Nehemiah is dealt with in lecture 3 (see especially note 1 of that lecture).

8. See Freedman 1961.

9. The suggestion of B. Halpern may be found in his essay, "Sacred History and Ideology: Chronicles' Thematic Structure—Indications of an Earlier Source" in Friedman 1981b, 35–54.

10. For these three books (Haggai, Zechariah, and Malachi) and prophets/prophecy during the period of restoration, see generally, Ackroyd 1968, 138–217; Mason 1977 and his essay in Coggins, Phillips, and Knibb 1982, 137–54; Blenkinsopp 1983, 225–42; Petersen 1977 and 1984; Barton 1986; Coggins 1987; and Meyers and Meyers 1987.

11. For discussions (with further bibliography) of the dates proposed for these two biblical books (Joel and Jonah), see Wolff 1977; Stuart 1987; and Sasson 1990.

12. For one scholar's attempt to address the vexing question of why the canonical prophets are virtually absent from the D-Work, see the series of articles by Begg (1985, 1986, and 1987).

13. See Freedman 1987 for this eighth-century collection. The biblical books Hosea and Amos are dealt with in detail in the commentaries of Andersen and Freedman 1980 and 1989. For Micah, see Mays 1976 and Wolff 1989. First Isaiah is treated extensively in Wildberger 1965–82 (note also Kaiser 1974 and 1983, and Hayes and Irvine 1987).

14. In addition to the usual array of journal articles, both Jeremiah and Ezekiel have in recent years been favored with the publication of major commentaries: Zimmerli (1979–83) and Greenberg (1983) on Ezekiel (note the review of these two works by J. Levenson in *Interpretation* 38 [1984], 210–17), and Carroll (1986), McKane (1986), and Holladay (1986–89) on Jeremiah. Holladay has provided a summary of his views on Jeremiah's life and work in *Jeremiah: A Fresh Reading* (New York: The Pilgrim Press, 1990).

15. On the varying orders of the major prophetic books in Jewish and Christian tradition, see Beckwith 1985, 181–211. This otherwise useful (and detailed) monograph is unfortunately hampered by the author's overt theological presuppositions, i.e., in the final analysis, the New Testament becomes the standard by which all other evidence is, and must be, measured (see, e.g., pp. 4–5, 10–12).

16. For the dates in Ezekiel, see Freedy and Redford 1970 (with slight modifications in their dates for the Egyptian twenty-sixth dynasty),

Greenberg 1983, 8–11, and the recent monograph of E. Kutsch, *Die chronologischen Daten des Ezechielbuches*, Orbus biblicus et orientalis 62 (Freiburg: Universitätsverlag, 1985).

17. For the chronological options, see Hayes and Miller 1977, 678–81. In general, the matter of a coherent chronology for the kings of Israel and Judah is a very messy business and one that usually bewilders the uninitiated. For orientation, see E. R. Thiele, *The Mysterious Numbers of the Hebrew Kings*, 3d ed. (Grand Rapids: Zondervan, 1983); and J. H. Hayes and P. K. Hooker, *A New Chronology for the Kings of Israel and Judah and its Implications for Biblical History and Literature* (Atlanta: John Knox Press, 1988).

18. For the question of a Third Isaiah (both for and against its existence), see Zimmerli 1950; Smart 1965, 13–39, 228–39; Westermann 1969, 295–308; Kaufmann 1970, 66–94; Blenkinsopp 1983, 242–51; and Soggin 1989, 391–97. Sekine 1989 provides a detailed examination of these chapters (56–66) from the standpoint of their redactional history. Note also the recent study of Koenan (1990).

19. On the historical context and history of scholarship concerning First Isaiah (chaps. 1–33, 36–39), see Wildberger 1965–82, Dietrich 1976, and Hayes and Irvine 1987. The latter argue for the substantial unity of chapters 1–33 (note also their brief review of scholarship on pp. 387–400). A popular, but still quite useful, introduction to the various scholarly "Isaiahs" and the continuity among them is W. L. Holladay's *Isaiah: Scroll of a Prophetic Heritage* (New York: The Pilgrim Press, 1978).

20. See Andersen and Freedman 1989, 183 passim.

21. As scholars have generally recognized, the reemergence of the Assyrian Empire during this period undoubtedly played a key role in the classical prophets' interest in political and military affairs beyond the borders of Israel and Judah. See Gottwald 1964, 94–146; Holladay 1970; Andersen and Freedman 1980, 31–44; and Blenkinsopp 1983, 80–137.

22. On the invasion of Sennacherib, see the recent commentary of Cogan and Tadmor 1988, 223–51; Clements 1980; and the earlier treatment of Childs 1967.

23. For the biblical accounts of this period, see 2 Kings 24–25, 2 Chronicles 36:5–21, and the relevant portions of the commentaries (Cogan and Tadmor 1988 and Williamson 1982).

24. On the question of the date of Malachi, see the recent linguistic analysis of A. Hill (in Meyers and O'Connor 1983, 77–89).

25. On the detection of Deuteronomistic elements in Genesis through Numbers, see the summary discussion in Soggin 1989, 143–45. Over the years, a number of scholars have advocated the addition of Joshua to the Pentateuch, thus forming a narrative unit known as the "Hexateuch" (see Wellhausen 1899; Driver 1913, 103–59; von Rad 1966, 1–93, 1947–48, and

1972, 13–24; contrast Noth 1987 [1957], 107–41, 174–87). For traces of P in the Former Prophets, see Hayes 1979, 200–206. Auld (1980) provides a history of the scholarly debate.

26. Jeremiah's priestly lineage, presumably reaching as far back as Abiathar, and his connection with the priests of Shilo are discussed in Bright 1965, lxxxviii, and Friedman 1987, 122–27. We agree with Friedman's views (1987, 117–35) concerning the Shilonite priests and the composition of the Deuteronomistic History.

27. For the various accounts in the Babylonian Talmud, see *Shabbath* 13b, 30b, and *Hagigah* 13a (the texts are conveniently collected in Lieman 1976, 72–73).

Lecture 3

1. Scholarly opinion is divided over the question of authorship of 1–2 Chronicles and Ezra-Nehemiah. The long-standing traditional view of common authorship has been challenged over the past decade or so with a number of prominent scholars arguing for two separate works, as opposed to one originally larger composition that later underwent secondary division. For discussion, see Freedman 1961; Japhet 1968; Williamson 1977, 5–70, and 1982, 5–11; Thronveit 1982; Ackroyd 1988; Blenkinsopp 1988, 47–54; and Talshir 1988.

2. On the various orders of the books within the Writings, see Patton 1908, 1–3, and Beckwith 1985, 181–211.

3. Rabbinic tradition (Babylonian Talmud, *Baba Bathra* 14a–15b) assigned the Book of Job to Moses (see Gordis 1965, 216; text in Leiman 1976, 52–53). Also, in the Syriac version of the Scriptures (the Peshitta), Job is placed immediately after the Pentateuch, implying Mosaic authorship. The Solomonic and/or Davidic connections within the other books are discussed in Meade 1987, 44–71.

4. For questions of authorship and date in the Book of Daniel, see the introductory discussions within the commentaries of Montgomery 1927, Hartman and Di Lella 1978, and, most recently, Goldingay 1989. Note also Bickermann 1967, 53–138, and Meade 1987, 85–91.

5. As an example, one might cite the book Qohelet (Ecclesiastes), for which W. F. Albright (influenced in part by the work of M. Dahood) later preferred a fifth-century B.C.E. date (see his *Yahweh and the Gods of Canaan* [Garden City, N.Y.: Doubleday, 1968], 261). Most scholars, however, generally place the time of composition in the third century B.C.E. (e.g., Bickermann 1967, 141; Hengel 1974, 1:115–16; Whybray 1989, 4–12; and Murphy 1990, 49, 172–73; contrast Whitley [1979, 132–48]), who argues for a second-century date).

6. See his *Against Apion* 1.7–8 (37–43) in *Josephus I: The Life; Against Apion*, trans. H. J. Thackeray, Loeb Classical Library (London and Cambridge: William Heinemann and Harvard University, 1926), 176–81.

7. On acrostic poems in the Hebrew Bible (e.g., Psalms 25, 34, 37, 119, 135; Proverbs 31:10–31; Lamentations 1–4), see Freedman 1980, 51–76, and 1986. The suggestion relating to the significance of a twenty-third line, as one finds, for example, in Psalms 25 and 34, was made by P. W. Skehan in "The Structure of the Song of Moses in Deuteronomy (Dt 32:1–43)," pp. 67–77 in his *Studies in Israelite Poetry and Wisdom*, CBQ Monograph Series 1 (Washington, D.C.: Catholic Biblical Association, 1971).

8. For this period as a whole—its religious communities and the texts produced by them—see generally Nickelsburg 1981; Stone 1984; Cohen 1987; and the magisterial revision of the older classic of Emil Schürer (revised by Vermes et al., see Schürer 1973–87). (See also note 23 below.)

9. Haran (1986) correctly recognizes that the repetition results from the breaking up of a larger work. However, he does not consider those manuscripts that place Chronicles at the head of the Writings. Note also Beckwith (1985: 211, 222), whose views on the position of Chronicles (always at the end of the Canon) are motivated more by his desire to confirm the New Testament evidence.

10. For the various themes of the Chronicler, see the earlier discussion of Freedman 1961 and the articles of Williamson (Williamson 1982, xviii–xix provides a partial listing). Note also especially Williamson 1977 and the seminal work of S. Japhet (1989 [1977]).

11. For connections between the Psalter and 1–2 Chronicles, see Driver 1913, 369–70, and Childs 1979, 514–15.

12. See the commentary of McKane (1970) on Proverbs and the general discussion of the various themes of this type of literature in Crenshaw 1981 and Murphy 1990. For the existence of schools in ancient Israel, see the recent review of the question in Crenshaw 1985.

13. See, e.g., Soggin 1989, 458–59 (tentative). For a brief review of the various approaches to the meaning of the book, see Childs 1979, 560–68, and Niditch in Knight and Tucker 1985, 453–54.

14. On the tradition of Solomonic authorship of these books, see Meade 1987, 53–62. The rather colorful history of the interpretation of Song of Songs (or Song of Solomon) is dealt with at length in Pope 1977, 89–229.

15. See the introductory discussion of this biblical book in Moore 1971, xvi–lx.

16. This is with the possible exception of an individual by the name of Elnathan, a governor of Judah (following Zerubbabel?), whose existence we know of through extra-biblical epigraphic evidence. Elnathan

had apparently married into the Davidic line through his wife Shelomith, a daughter of Zerrubabel (1 Chronicles 3:19). For discussion, see N. Avigad, *Bullae and Seals from a Post-exilic Judean Archive*, Qedem 4 (Jerusalem: The Hebrew University Institute of Archaeology, 1976); Meyers 1985; Meyers and Meyers 1987, 12–14; and Williamson 1988, 70–76.

17. See note 1 of this lecture for references relevant to this discussion.

18. The issues surrounding the interpretation of this difficult verse are outlined in the commentary of Williamson (1985, 357, 364–65).

19. On the Book of Job in general and the problems it raises for the modern interpreter, see Pope 1965; Glatzer 1969; Habel 1985; Freedman 1988; and, most recently, Clines 1989.

20. Note in this regard the earlier article of Tsevat, who contends that "the solution which the book offers to the problem [of Job's suffering] is the radical denial of the principle of retribution" (1966, 101; see also 98–100).

21. For this biblical book (Daniel), see the references in note 4 of this lecture.

22. For a general introduction to this genre (apocalyptic), see Russell 1964; Stone 1984, 383–441; and Collins 1977 (on Daniel) and 1987.

23. Translations of the Apocrypha may be found in *The New Oxford Annotated Bible with the Apocrypha, Revised Standard Version*, expanded edition (New York: Oxford University Press, 1977). For the Pseudepigrapha, see *The Old Testament Pseudepigrapha*, 2 vols., ed. J. H. Charlesworth (New York: Doubleday, 1983–85).

Of particular interest in relation to the Book of Daniel are the "Prayer of Nabonidus" (the last king of the Neo-Babylonian or "Chaldean" dynasty) and the Pseudo-Danielic writings, both from Cave 4 at Qumran (see Vermes 1987: 274–75). The former parallels the story of the cure of Nebuchadnezzar in Daniel 4, except that Nabonidus is cured by a Jewish exorcist (see Freedman 1957 and Cross 1984), while the latter apparently refers, like Daniel, to four kingdoms and even uses the terms *Son of God* and *Son of the Most High* (see Schürer 1973–87, vol. 3, pt. 1, p. 442).

24. The additions to Daniel are translated with commentary in Moore 1977, 23–149. For the literature of Qumran (the Dead Sea Scrolls), see generally Schürer 1973–87, vol. 3, pt. 1, pp. 380–469, and Vermes 1987.

Abbreviations

AB   Anchor Bible
ATANT   Abhandlungen zur Theologie des Alten und Neuen Testaments
BibRev *Bible Review*
BASOR   *Bulletin of the American Schools of Oriental Research*
CBQ   *Catholic Biblical Quarterly*
EI   *Eretz-Israel*
FRLANT Forschungen zur Religion und Literatur des Alten und Neuen Testaments
HSM   Harvard Semitic Monographs
HTR   *Harvard Theological Review*
HUCA   *Hebrew Union College Annual*
ICC   International Critical Commentary
IDB   *Interpreter's Dictionary of the Bible*
JANES   *Journal of the Ancient Near Eastern Society*
JAOS   *Journal of the American Oriental Society*
JBL   *Journal of Biblical Literature*
JJS   *Journal of Jewish Studies*
JSOT   *Journal for the Study of the Old Testament*
NCBC   New Century Bible Commentary
OTL   Old Testament Library

Abbreviations

RB	*Revue Biblique*
SBLMS	Society of Biblical Literature Monograph Series
SBT	Studies in Biblical Theology
VT	*Vetus Testamentum*
VTSup	Supplements to *Vetus Testamentum*
WBC	Word Biblical Commentary
ZAW	*Zeitschrift für die alttestamentliche Wissenschaft*

Bibliography

Prepared by John R. Huddlestun

Ackroyd, P. R. 1968. *Exile and Restoration*. OTL. Philadelphia: Westminster Press.
———. 1987. *Studies in the Religious Tradition of the Old Testament*. London: SCM Press.
———. 1988. Chronicles-Ezra-Nehemiah: The Concept of Unity. *ZAW* 100 (Supp.): 189–201.
Andersen, F. I., and Freedman, D. N. 1980. *Hosea*. AB 24. New York: Doubleday.
———. 1989. *Amos*. AB 24a. New York: Doubleday.
Auld, A. G. 1980. *Joshua, Moses and the Land: Tetrateuch-Pentateuch-Hexateuch in a Generation Since 1938*. Edinburgh: T. and T. Clark.
Barton, J. 1986. *Oracles of God. Perceptions of Ancient Prophecy in Israel After the Exile*. New York and Oxford: Oxford University Press.
Beckwith, R. T. 1985. *The Old Testament Canon of the New Testament Church and its Background in Early Judaism*. Grand Rapids, Mich.: Eerdmans.
Begg, C. 1985. A Bible Mystery: The Absence of Jeremiah in the Deuteronomistic History. *Irish Biblical Studies* 7:139–64.
———. 1986. The Non-Mention of Amos, Hosea, and Micah in the Deuteronomistic History. *Biblische Notizen* 32:41–53.
———. 1987. The Non-Mention of Zephaniah, Nahum, and Habakkuk in the Deuteronomistic History. *Biblische Notizen* 38–39:19–25.
Bickermann, E. 1967. *Four Strange Books of the Bible: Jonah, Daniel, Kohelet, Esther*. New York: Schocken Books.
———. 1988. *The Jews in the Greek Age*. Cambridge, Mass.: Harvard University Press.

Bibliography

Blenkinsopp, J. 1983. *A History of Prophecy in Israel*. Philadelphia: Westminster Press.

———. 1988. *Ezra-Nehemiah*. OTL. Philadelphia: Westminster Press.

Bright, J. 1965. *Jeremiah*. AB 21. New York: Doubleday.

———. 1981. *A History of Israel*. 3d ed. Philadelphia: Westminster Press.

Brooks, R. 1990. *The Spirit of the Ten Commandments: Shattering the Myth of Rabbinic Legalism*. San Francisco: Harper and Row.

Campbell, E. F. 1975. *Ruth*. AB 7. New York: Doubleday.

Carmichael, C. M. 1985. *Law and Narrative in the Bible: The Evidence of the Deuteronomic Laws and the Decalogue*. Ithaca and London: Cornell University Press.

Carroll, R. P. 1986. *Jeremiah*. OTL. Philadelphia: Westminster Press.

Childs, B. S. 1967. *Isaiah and the Assyrian Crisis*. SBT, 2d Ser. 3. London: SCM Press.

———. 1970. *Biblical Theology in Crisis*. Philadelphia: Westminster Press.

———. 1974. *The Book of Exodus. A Critical, Theological Commentary*. OTL. Philadelphia: Westminster Press.

———. 1979. *Introduction to the Old Testament as Scripture*. Philadelphia: Westminster Press. [Note the scholarly response to this volume in *JSOT* 16 (1980): 1–60.]

Clements, R. E. 1976. *One Hundred Years of Old Testament Interpretation*. Philadelphia: Westminster Press.

———. 1980. *Isaiah and the Deliverance of Jerusalem*. JSOT Supp. Ser. 13. Sheffield, Eng.: JSOT Press.

Clines, D. J. A. 1978. *The Theme of the Pentateuch*. JSOT Supp. Ser. 10. Sheffield, Eng.: JSOT Press.

———. 1989. *Job 1–20*. WBC 17. Dallas: Word Books.

Cogan, M., and Tadmor, H. 1988. *II Kings*. AB 11. New York: Doubleday.

Coggins, R. J. 1987. *Haggai, Zechariah, Malachi*. Old Testament Guides. Sheffield, Eng.: JSOT Press.

Coggins, R., Phillips, A., and Knibb, M., eds. 1982. *Israel's Prophetic Tradition. Essays in Honour of Peter Ackroyd*. Cambridge: Cambridge University Press.

Cohen, S. J. D. 1987. *From the Maccabees to the Mishnah*. Library of Early Christianity 7. Philadelphia: Westminster Press.

Collins, J. J. 1977. *The Apocalyptic Vision of the Book of Daniel*. HSM 16. Missoula, Mont.: Scholars Press.

———. 1987. *The Apocalyptic Imagination*. New York: Crossroad.

Crenshaw, J. L. 1981. *Old Testament Wisdom. An Introduction*. Atlanta: John Knox Press.

———. 1985. Education in Ancient Israel. *JBL* 104:601–15.

Bibliography

Cross, F. M. 1973. *Canaanite Myth and Hebrew Epic.* Cambridge, Mass.: Harvard University Press.

———. 1984. The Prayer of Nabonidus. *Israel Exploration Journal* 34:260–64.

Davies, W. D., and Finkelstein, L., eds. 1984. *The Cambridge History of Judaism.* Vol. 1. *Introduction; Persian Period.* Cambridge: Cambridge University Press.

Dearman, J. A. 1990. My Servants the Scribes: Composition and Context in Jeremiah 36. *JBL* 109:403–21.

de Vaux, R. 1971. *The Bible and the Ancient Near East.* Trans. by D. McHugh of selected essays from *Bible et Orient* (1967). New York: Doubleday.

Dietrich, W. 1972. *Prophetie und Geschichte. Eine redaktionsgeschichtliche Untersuchung zum deuteronomistischen Geschichtswerk.* FRLANT 108. Göttingen: Vandenhoeck and Ruprecht.

———. 1976. *Jesaja und die Politik.* Beiträge zur evangelischen Theologie 74. Munich: Chr. Kaiser.

Driver, S. R. 1913. *An Introduction to the Literature of the Old Testament.* 9th ed. Edinburgh: T. and T. Clark.

Eissfeldt, O. 1965. *The Old Testament. An Introduction.* Trans. P. R. Ackroyd from German, 3d ed., 1964. New York: Harper and Row.

Firmage, E. B., Weiss, B. G., and Welch, J. W. eds. 1990. *Religion and Law: Biblical-Judaic Perspectives.* Winona Lake, Ind.: Eisenbrauns.

Freedman, D. N. 1957. The Prayer of Nabonidus. *BASOR* 145: 31–32.

———. 1961. The Chronicler's Purpose. *CBQ* 23: 436–42.

———. 1962. Pentateuch. In *IDB*, 3:711–27. Nashville: Abingdon.

———. 1963. The Law and the Prophets. In VTSup 9:250–65. Leiden: E. J. Brill.

———. 1975. Son of Man, Can These Bones Live? *Interpretation* 29: 171–86.

———. 1976a. Canon of the Old Testament. In *IDB Supplementary Volume,* 130–36. Nashville: Abingdon.

———. 1976b. Deuteronomic History. In *IDB Supplementary Volume,* 226–28. Nashville: Abingdon.

———. 1980. *Pottery, Poetry, and Prophecy: Studies in Early Hebrew Poetry.* Winona Lake, Ind.: Eisenbrauns.

———. 1983a. The Earliest Bible. *Michigan Quarterly Review* 22, no. 3 (Summer): 167–75.

———. 1983b. The Spelling of the Name "David" in the Hebrew Bible. *Hebrew Annual Review* 7:89–104.

———. 1986. Acrostic Poems in the Hebrew Bible: Alphabetic and Otherwise. *CBQ* 48:408–31.

———. 1987. Headings in the Books of the Eighth-Century Prophets. *Andrews University Seminary Studies* 25:9–26.

———. 1988. Is it Possible to Understand the Book of Job? *BibRev* 4, no. 2:26–33, 44.

———. 1989. The Nine Commandments. The Secret Progress of Israel's Sins. *BibRev* 5, no. 6:28–37, 42.

———. 1990. The Formation of the Canon of the Old Testament. In Firmage, Weiss, and Welch 1990, 315–31.

Freedy, K. S., and Redford, D. B. 1970. The Dates in Ezekiel in Relation to Biblical, Babylonian and Egyptian Sources. *JAOS* 90:462–85.

Freund, R. A. 1989. Murder, Adultery and Theft? *Scandinavian Journal of the Old Testament* 2:72–80.

Friedman, R. E. 1981a. *The Exile and Biblical Narrative: The Formation of the Deuteronomistic and Priestly Works.* HSM 22. Chico, Calif.: Scholars Press.

———. 1987. *Who Wrote the Bible?* New York: Summit Books.

———, ed. 1981b. *The Creation of Sacred Literature. Composition and Redaction of the Biblical Text.* Berkeley: University of California Press.

Glatzer, N., ed. 1969. *The Dimensions of Job.* New York: Schocken Books.

Goldingay, J. E. 1989. *Daniel.* WBC 30. Dallas: Word Books.

Gordis, R. 1965. *The Book of God and Man: A Study of Job.* Chicago: University of Chicago Press.

Gottwald, N. K. 1964. *All the Kingdoms of the Earth. Israelite Prophecy and International Relations in the Ancient Near East.* New York: Harper and Row.

Greenberg, M. 1971. Decalogue. In *Encyclopedia Judaica,* vol. 5, cols. 1435–46. New York and Jerusalem: Macmillan and Keter Publishing.

———. 1983. *Ezekiel, 1–20.* AB 22. New York: Doubleday.

Habel, N. C. 1985. *The Book of Job.* OTL. Philadelphia: Westminster Press.

Halpern, B. 1988. *The First Historians. The Hebrew Bible and History.* San Francisco: Harper and Row.

Halpern, B., and Levenson, J. D., eds. 1981. *Traditions in Transformation: Turning Points in Biblical Faith.* Winona Lake, Ind.: Eisenbrauns.

Haran, M. 1981. Behind the Scenes of History: Determining the Date of the Priestly Source. *JBL* 100:321–33.

———. 1985. Book Size and the Device of Catch-Lines in the Biblical Canon. *JJS* 36:1–11.

———. 1986. Explaining the Individual Lines at the End of Chronicles and the Beginning of Ezra. *BibRev* 2, no. 3:18–20.

Hartman, L. F., and Alexander, A. D. L. 1978. *The Book of Daniel.* AB 23. New York: Doubleday.

Hayes, J. H. 1979. *An Introduction to Old Testament Study.* Nashville: Abingdon.

Hayes, J. H., and Irvine, S. A. 1987. *Isaiah the Eighth-Century Prophet.* Nashville: Abingdon.

Hayes, J. H., and Miller, J. M., eds. 1977. *Israelite and Judean History.* Philadelphia: Westminster.

Hengel, M. 1974. *Judaism and Hellenism: Studies in their Encounter in Palestine during the Early Hellenistic Period.* 2 vols. Trans. by J. Bowden from *Judentum und Hellenismus*, 2d rev. ed. (1973). Philadelphia: Fortress Press.

Herrmann, S. 1981. *A History of Israel in Old Testament Times.* Rev. and enl. 2d ed. Philadelphia: Fortress.

Hoffmann, H.-D. 1980. *Reform und Reformen: Untersuchungen zu einem Grundthema der deuteronomistischen Geschichtsschreibung.* ATANT 66. Zurich: Theologischer Verlag.

Holladay, J. S. 1970. Assyrian Statecraft and the Prophets of Israel. *HTR* 63:29–51.

Holladay, W. L. 1986–89. *Jeremiah 1 and 2.* 2 vols. Hermeneia. Philadelphia and Minneapolis: Fortress Press.

Hölscher, G. 1952. *Geschichtsschreibung in Israel: Untersuchungen zum Jahvisten und Elohisten.* Skrifter utgivna av kungl. Humanistiska Vetenskapssamfundet i Lund 50. Lund: Gleerup.

Houtman, C. 1981. Ezra and the Law. *Oudtestamentische Studiën* 21:91–115.

Hurvitz, A. 1974. The Evidence of Language in Dating the Priestly Code. *RB* 81:24–56.

―――. 1982. *A Linguistic Study of the Relationship between the Priestly Source and the Book of Ezekiel.* Cahiers de la *RB* 20. Paris: Gabalda.

―――. 1988. Dating the Priestly Source in Light of the Historical Study of Biblical Hebrew a Century after Wellhausen. *ZAW* 100 (Supp.): 88–100.

Japhet, S. 1968. The Supposed Common Authorship of Chronicles and Ezra-Nehemiah Investigated Anew. *VT* 18:330–71.

―――. 1989. *The Ideology of the Book of Chronicles and Its Place in Biblical Thought.* Trans. from Hebrew, 1977. Frankfurt am Main: Peter Lang.

Kaiser, O. 1974. *Isaiah 13–39.* Trans. from German, 1973. OTL. Philadelphia: Westminster Press.

―――. 1983. *Isaiah 1–12.* 2d ed. Trans. from German, 1981. OTL. Philadelphia: Westminster Press.

Kaufman, S. A. 1979. The Structure of the Deuteronomic Law. *Maarav* 1:105–58.

Kaufmann, Y. 1960. *The Religion of Israel From its Beginnings to the Babylonian Exile.* Trans. and abr. by M. Greenberg from Hebrew *Toledot Ha-Emunah Ha-Yisraelit*, 1937–48. New York: Schocken Books.

―――. 1970. *The Babylonian Captivity and Deutero-Isaiah.* Trans. by C. W.

Bibliography

Efroymson from Hebrew *Toledot Ha-Emunah Ha-Yisraelit* (1956), vol. 4, bk. 1, chaps. 1–2. New York: Union of American Hebrew Congregations.

Kellermann, U. 1968. Erwägungen zum Esragesetz. *ZAW* 80:373–85.

Klein, R. W. 1979. *Israel in Exile. A Theological Interpretation.* Overtures to Biblical Theology. Philadelphia: Fortress Press.

Knight, D. A., ed. 1983. *Julius Wellhausen and His* Prolegomena to the History of Israel. Semeia 25. Chico, Calif.: Scholars Press.

Knight, D. A., and Tucker, G. M., eds. 1985. *The Hebrew Bible and its Modern Interpreters.* Chico, Calif.: Scholars Press.

Knohl, I. 1987. The Priestly Torah Versus the Holiness School: Sabbath and the Festivals. *HUCA* 58:65–117.

Koenen, K. 1990. *Ethik und Eschatologie im Tritojesajabuch.* Wissenschaftliche Monographien zum Alten und Neuen Testament 62. Neukirchen-Vluyn: Neukirchener Verlag.

Leiman, S. Z. 1976. *The Canonization of Hebrew Scripture: The Talmudic and Midrashic Evidence.* Transactions of the Connecticut Academy of Arts and Sciences 47. Hamden, Conn.: Archon Books.

———, ed. 1974. *The Canon and Masorah of the Hebrew Bible. An Introductory Reader.* New York: KTAV Publishing House.

Mays, J. L. 1976. *Micah.* OTL. Philadelphia: Westminster Press.

McKane, W. 1970. *Proverbs. A New Approach.* OTL. Philadelphia: Westminster.

———. 1986. *A Critical and Exegetical Commentary on Jeremiah*, vol. 1 (Jeremiah 1–25). ICC. Edinburgh: T. and T. Clark.

McKenzie, S. L. 1984. *The Chronicler's Use of the Deuteronomic History.* HSM 33. Decatur, Ga.: Scholars Press. [Note review by P. B. Dirksen in *Bibliotheca Orientalis* 44 (1987): 218–22.]

Meade, D. G. 1987. *Pseudonymity and Canon.* Grand Rapids, Mich.: Eerdmans.

Meyers, E. M. 1985. The Shelomith Seal and the Judean Restoration. Some Additional Considerations. In *EI* 18 (Nahman Avigad vol.), 33*–38*. Jerusalem: Israel Exploration Society.

Meyers, C. L., and Myers, E. M. 1987. *Haggai, Zechariah 1–8.* AB 25b. New York: Doubleday.

Meyers, C. L., and O'Connor, M., eds. 1983. *The Word of the Lord Shall Go Forth. Essays in Honor of David Noel Freedman in Celebration of His Sixtieth Birthday.* Winona Lake, Ind.: Eisenbrauns.

Miller, J. M., and Hayes, J. H. 1986. *A History of Ancient Israel and Judah.* Philadelphia: Westminster Press.

Montgomery, J. A. 1927. *A Critical and Exegetical Commentary on the Book of Daniel.* ICC. Edinburgh: T. and T. Clark.

Moore, C. A. 1971. *Esther*. AB 7b. New York: Doubleday.

————. 1977. *Daniel, Esther, and Jeremiah: The Additions*. AB 44. New York: Doubleday.

Moran, W. J. 1967. The Conclusion of the Decalogue (Ex 20,17 = Dt 5,21). *CBQ* 29:543–54.

Muilenburg, J. 1970. Baruch the Scribe. In *Proclamation and Presence. Old Testament Essays in Honour of Gwynne Henton Davies*, ed. J. I. Durham and J. R. Porter, 215–38. Richmond, Va.: John Knox Press.

Murphy, R. E. 1990. *The Tree of Life: An Exploration of Biblical Wisdom Literature*. Anchor Bible Reference Library. New York: Doubleday.

Nelson, R. D. 1981. *The Double Redaction of the Deuteronomic History*. JSOT Supp. Ser. 18. Sheffield, Eng.: JSOT Press.

Newsome, J. D. 1979. *By the Waters of Babylon. An Introduction to the History and Theology of the Exile*. Atlanta: John Knox Press.

Nickelsburg, G. W. E. 1981. *Jewish Literature Between the Bible and the Mishnah*. Philadelphia: Fortress Press.

Nielsen, E. 1968. *The Ten Commandments in New Perspective*. SBT, 2d Ser. 7. Trans. by D. J. Bourke from German, 1965. Naperville, Ill.: Allenson.

Noth, M. 1972. *A History of Pentateuchal Traditions*. Trans. by B. W. Anderson from German, 1948. Englewood Cliffs, N.J.: Prentice-Hall. Reprint. Chico, Calif.: Scholars Press, 1981.

————. 1981. *The Deuteronomic History*. Trans. J. Doull et. al. JSOT Supp. Ser. 15. Sheffield: JSOT Press. Trans. from *Überlieferungsgeschichtliche Studien*. 2d ed., pp. 1–110. Tubingen: Max Niemeyer Verlag, 1957. 1st ed., 1943.

————. 1987. *The Chronicler's History*. Trans. H. G. M. Williamson. JSOT Supp. Ser. 50. Sheffield, Eng.: JSOT Press. Trans. from *Überlieferungsgeschichtliche Studien*, 2d ed., pp. 110–216. Tübingen: Max Niemeyer Verlag, 1957. 1st ed., 1943.

O'Brien, M. A. 1989. *The Deuteronomistic History Hypothesis: A Reassessment*. Orbis biblicus et orientalis 92. Göttingen: Vandenhoeck and Ruprecht.

Overholt, T. W. 1989. *Channels of Prophecy. The Social Dynamics of Prophetic Activity*. Minneapolis, Minn.: Fortress Press.

Paton, L. B. 1908. *The Book of Esther*. ICC. Edinburgh: T. and T. Clark.

Peckham, B. 1985. *The Composition of the Deuteronomistic History*. HSM 35. Atlanta: Scholars Press.

Perdue, L. G., and Kovacs, B. W., eds. 1984. *A Prophet to the Nations: Essays in Jeremiah Studies*. Winona Lake, Ind.: Eisenbrauns.

Petersen, D. L. 1977. *Late Israelite Prophecy: Studies in Deutero-Prophetic Literature and in Chronicles*. SBLMS 23. Atlanta: Scholars Press.

Bibliography

──────. 1984. *Haggai and Zechariah 1–8*. OTL. Philadelphia: Westminster Press.

Phillips, A. 1970. *Ancient Israel's Criminal Law: A New Approach to the Decalogue*. New York: Schocken Books.

Polzin, R. 1976. *Late Biblical Hebrew: Toward an Historical Typology of Biblical Hebrew Prose*. HSM 12. Missoula, Mont.: Scholars Press.

Pope, M. 1965. *Job*. AB 15. New York: Doubleday.

──────. 1977. *Song of Songs*. AB 7c. New York: Doubleday.

Provan, 1988. *Hezekiah and the Book of Kings: A Contribution to the Debate about the Composition of the Deuteronomistic History*. Beiheft zur ZAW 172. Berlin: Walter de Gruyter.

Rad, G. von. 1947–48. Hexateuch oder Pentateuch? *Verkundigung und Forschung* 1–2:52–55.

──────. 1966. *The Problem of the Hexateuch and Other Essays*. Trans. by E. W. T. Dicken from German *Gesammelte Studien zum Alten Testament*, 1958. Edinburgh: Oliver and Boyd.

──────. 1972. *Genesis. A Commentary*. Rev. ed. (based on German 9th ed., 1972). OTL. Philadelphia: Westminster Press.

Radjawane, A. N. 1973–74. Das deuteronomische Geschichtswerk: Ein Forschungsbericht. *Theologische Rundschau* 38:177–216.

Rendsburg, G. 1980. Late Biblical Hebrew and the Date of 'P'. *JANES* 12:65–80.

Rendtorff, R. 1977. *Das überlieferungsgeschichtliche Problem des Pentateuch*. Beiheft zur ZAW 147. Berlin and New York: Walter de Gruyter. [Note the scholarly response to this volume and Rendtorff's views in *JSOT* 3 (1977).]

──────. 1984. Esra und das "Gesetz." *ZAW* 96:165–84.

Rogerson, J. 1985. *Old Testament Criticism in the Nineteenth Century: England and Germany*. Philadelphia: Fortress Press.

Rowley, H. H. 1965. *The Servant of the Lord and Other Essays on the Old Testament*. 2d ed. Oxford: Basil Blackwell.

Russell, D. S. 1964. *The Method and Message of Jewish Apocalyptic 200 BC–AD 100*. OTL. Philadelphia: Westminster Press.

Sasson, J. M. 1979. *Ruth*. Baltimore: Johns Hopkins University Press.

──────. 1990. *Jonah*. AB 24b. New York: Doubleday.

Schmid, H. H. 1976. *Der sogenannte Jahwist: Beobachtungen und Fragen zur Pentateuchforschung*. Zurich: Theologischer Verlag.

Schürer, E. 1973–87. *The History of the Jewish People in the Age of Jesus Christ (175 B.C.–A.D. 35)*. 3 vols. Rev. and ed. G. Vermes, F. Millar, M. Black, M. Goodman, and P. Vermes. Edinburgh: T. and T. Clark.

Segal, B.-Z., and Levi, G., eds. 1990. *The Ten Commandments in History and Tradition*. Trans. from Hebrew, 1985. Jerusalem: Magnes Press.

Sekine, S. 1989. *Die Tritojesajanische Sammlung (Jes 56–66) redaktionsgeschichtlich untersucht.* Beiheft zur ZAW 175. Berlin and New York: Walter de Gruyter.

Smart, J. D. 1965. *History and Theology in Second Isaiah.* Philadelphia: Westminster.

Smend, R. 1971. Das Gesetz und die Völker: Ein Beitrag zur deuteronomistischen Redaktionsgeschichte. In *Probleme biblischer Theologie,* ed. H. W. Wolff, 494–509. Munich: Chr. Kaiser.

Smith, D. L. 1989. *The Religion of the Landless: The Social Context of the Babylonian Exile.* Bloomington, Ind.: Meyer-Stone Books.

Soggin, J. A. 1989. *Introduction to the Old Testament.* 3d ed. Trans. J. Bowden from Italian, 4th ed., 1987. OTL. Louisville, Ky.: Westminster/John Knox Press.

Stamm, J. J., and Andrew, M. E. 1967. *The Ten Commandments in Recent Research.* SBT, 2d Ser. 2. Naperville, Ill.: Allenson.

Stone, M., ed. 1984. *Jewish Writings of the Second Temple Period: Apocrypha, Pseudepigrapha, Qumran Sectarian Writings, Philo, Josephus.* Compendia Rerum Iudaicarum ad Novum Testamentum, Section Two. Assen, The Netherlands: Van Gorcum and Philadelphia: Fortress Press.

Stuart, D. 1987. *Hosea-Jonah.* WBC 31. Waco, Tex.: Word Books.

Talshir, D. 1988. A Reinvestigation of the Linguistic Relationship Between Chronicles and Ezra-Nehemiah. *VT* 38:165–93.

Thompson, R. J. 1970. *Moses and the Law in a Century of Criticism Since Graf.* VTSup 19. Leiden: E. J. Brill.

Thronveit, M. A. 1982. Linguistic Analysis and the Question of Authorship in Chronicles, Ezra, and Nehemiah. *VT* 32:201–16.

Tigay, J. H. 1975. An Empirical Basis for the Documentary Hypothesis. *JBL* 94:329–42.

———., ed. 1985. *Empirical Models for Biblical Criticism.* Philadelphia: University of Pennsylvania Press.

Tsevat, M. 1966. The Meaning of the Book of Job. *HUCA* 37: 73–106.

Van Seters, J. 1983. *In Search of History. Historiography in the Ancient World and the Origins of Biblical History.* New Haven and London: Yale University Press.

Vermes, G. 1987. *The Dead Sea Scrolls in English.* 3d ed. London: Penguin Books.

Vink, J. G. 1969. The Date and Origin of the Priestly Code in the Old Testament. *Oudtestamentische Studiën* 15:1–144.

Weinfeld, M. 1972. *Deuteronomy and the Deuteronomic School.* New York: Oxford University Press.

———. 1990. The Decalogue: Its Significance, Uniqueness, and Place in Israel's Tradition. In Firmage, Weiss, and Welch 1990, 3–47.

Wellhausen, J. 1885. *Prolegomena to the History of Ancient Israel*. Trans. from *Prolegomena zur Geschichte Israels*, 2d ed. (1883) by J. S. Black and A. Menzies. Edinburgh: Adam and Charles Black. Reprint. New York: Meridan Books, 1957.

———. 1899. *Die Composition des Hexateuchs und der historischen Bücher des Alten Testaments*. 3d ed. Berlin: Georg Reimer.

Westermann, C. 1969. *Isaiah 40–66*. Trans. from German, 1966. OTL. Philadelphia: Westminster Press.

White, S. A. 1990. The All Souls Deuteronomy and the Decalogue. *JBL* 109:193–206.

Whitley, C. F. 1979. *Kohelet: His Language and Thought*. Beiheft zur ZAW 148. Berlin: Walter de Gruyter.

Whybray, R. N. 1987. *The Making of the Pentateuch. A Methodological Study*. JSOT Supp. Ser. 53. Sheffield: Sheffield Academic Press.

———. 1989. *Ecclesiastes*. NCBC. London and Grand Rapids, Mich.: Marshall, Morgan and Scott and Eerdmans.

Wildberger, H. 1965–82. *Jesaja 1–39*. Biblischer Kommentar—Altes Testament, X.1–3. Neukirchen-Vluyn: Neukirchener Verlag.

Williamson, H. G. M. 1977. *Israel in the Books of Chronicles*. Cambridge: Cambridge University Press.

———. 1982. *1 and 2 Chronicles*. NCBC. Grand Rapids, Mich.: Eerdmans.

———. 1985. *Ezra, Nehemiah*. WBC 16. Waco, Tex.: Word Books.

———. 1987. *Ezra and Nehemiah*. Old Testament Guides. Sheffield: JSOT Press.

———. 1988. The Governors of Judah under the Persians. *Tyndale Bulletin* 39:59–82.

Wilson, R. W. 1980. *Prophecy and Society in Ancient Israel*. Philadelphia: Fortress Press.

Wolff, H. W. 1961. Das Kerygma des deuteronomischen Geschichtswerk. *ZAW* 73:171–86. Trans. as The Kerygma of the Deuteronomic Historical Work. In *The Vitality of Old Testament Traditions*, ed. W. Brueggemann and H. W. Wolff. Atlanta: John Knox, 1975.

———. 1977. *Joel and Amos*. Trans. from German, 1975. Hermeneia. Philadelphia: Fortress Press.

———. 1989. *Micah, A Commentary*. Trans. from German, 1982. Minneapolis: Augsburg.

Zevit, Z. 1982. Converging Lines of Evidence Bearing on the Date of P. *ZAW* 94:502–9.

Zimmerli, W. 1950. Zur Sprache Tritojesajas. Schweizerische theologische Umschau 20:110–22.

―――. 1979–83. *Ezekiel 1 and 2*. 2 vols. Hermeneia. Philadelphia: Fortress Press.

DATE DUE

APR - 2 2016		
JUL 2 6 2016		

GAYLORD   #3523PI   Printed in USA